How to
Airbrush, Pinstripe &

Timothy Remus

Published by:
Wolfgang Publications Inc.
P.O. Box 223
Stillwater, MN 55082
www.wolfpub.com

Legals

First published in 2012 by Wolfgang Publications Inc.,
P.O. Box 223, Stillwater MN 55082

ISBN 13: 978-1-935828-69-3

Printed and bound in U.S.A.

How to Airbrush, Pinstripe & Goldleaf

Acknowledgements

This book is a compilation of how-to sequences done by a series of talented artists.

I'm blessed with a lot of friends, and luckily, some are very talented artists. The group represented here are a mix of old and new, and I'm grateful to each one for sharing some of their secrets with me – and ultimately with the readers. In no particular order, I want to thank each of the following:

Leah and Brian Gall. I found Leah and Brian Gall ten or more years ago painting away in a local shop, and since then they've helped me a number of times with airbrush and custom painting sequences, all of which ended up in a number of how-to-paint books.

Lenni Schwartz. Lenni might not have any hair, but he's got tons of talent and a great smile. Lenni is another of those who can do anything from complete paint jobs to airbrush, pinstripe and sign painting. And along the way, all of his talents have been illustrated in various Wolfgang books.

Tracy Hilgers. Tracy falls into the new friends category. Though he helped with the NEW Jon Kosmoski Kustom Painting Secrets book, it's only recently that I've come to know Tracy and appreciate his talents.

Dave Letterfly. Dave is another newbie to Wolfgang. It all came about during a winter trip to Florida. When my arrangement to shoot a sequence with a well-known Florida artist fell apart, I went to the local Harley dealer looking for a referral of sorts to the best pinstriper in the area. Thus I met Dave, and his side-kick Mike, and the Labrador. I have a great job.

Kelley St. Croix-Bush. Kelley St. Croix is a newbie to Wolfgang, though her husband, Bruce Bush, is another friend I can always count on to paint a sequence I need for a project, or help me find a new pinstripe or airbrush artist – in this case his talented wife Kelley.

Andy Anderson. Andy and I became friends in Daytona many moons ago when I went looking for the guy responsible for the killer paint job on a bike at the Boardwalk show. Since then he's helped with a couple of books and always comes through in a pinch.

John Hartnett. John is a new artist for Wolfgang, but an institution in the area south of Boston where he plies his trade. As luck would have it, I was able to mix business and pleasure when a visit to the Shadley Brothers shop, coincided with a goldleaf job John was doing on one of their bikes.

Mark Brodie. New to Wolfgang, Mark and I were stuck, so to speak, for a week at the same facility in Sturgis. Before long I was admiring one of his paint jobs, and before the week was out I had a complete start-to-finish pinstripe sequence safely tucked away on the 4-gig card in my trusty Canon.

Mickey Harris: Though Mickey may be the most famous artist in this fine tome, he's new to Wolfgang. Serendipity brought he and I together at the SATA facility in southern Minnesota. Google Mickey Harris, he's impressive.

Tex McDorman. Though he lives in Texas and I live in Minnesota, our paths seem to cross on a regular basis. As we became friends over the years Tex also became a contributor to Wolfgang. Tex is one of those guys who can stripe and talk and greet an old friend who just walked up to the booth, all at the same time – and crank out a lot of great work to boot.

I always say that no man is an island, and no author really does it alone. In my case I need to thank Deb Shade for contributing two chapters, and my huge staff of two (Jacki and Krista) for doing the layout and paying the bills respectively.

Introduction

The genesis of this book starts with a lunch conversation with one of the salesmen for the company that distributes my books to the big accounts like Barnes & Noble and Amazon. He pointed out the obvious, that while there have been numerous books about pinstriping, airbrushing, and goldleaf, no one he knew of ever combined the three art forms into one how-to book.

I'm sure I've told this story before, but when I worked as a mechanic there were of course times when I didn't know what the hell I was doing. How to put a new clutch assembly in a front wheel drive SAAB, or correctly repair the carburetor on some old Toyota (the one I'd already had apart three times). To find the answer, I went to the guy who knew more about Toyota carbs, or SAAB clutches than anyone else in the area.

So while it seems too obvious, I believe in teaching you how to pinstripe, airbrush and apply goldleaf, by showing you how the professionals do it. Not just any professionals, but the really good ones, the ones who've been doing it for years, the ones who I know will help with writing the captions so they can share with readers in words as well as photos what they've learned from doing hundreds and hundreds of paint jobs.

The book is broken down into ten chapters, each the property, so to speak, of one artist. The jobs themselves range from simple to complex, and many of them actually combine more than one of the three topics, i.e. the Lenni Schwartz project combines both goldleaf and pinstripe.

I like to think that there's something here for everyone, both the newbies and the veterans. A new spin on airbrushes, or a better way to hold the pinstripe brush while doing a tight turn. Really, this book is just a vehicle that allows one artist to share tips and tricks with hundreds of others – and that's got to be a good thing.

Chapter One

Lenni Schwartz

An Accent of Antique Goldleaf

Spending time observing Lenni create amazing works of art is more than just a pleasure - I consider it to be an honor. He has always graciously opened his doors and allowed my camera to capture him at his times of certain focus. After all, he may make it look easy to do, but as we all know it is not. It takes a lot of dedication to get to the

level he is at and he'll be the first to tell you there are no shortcuts to being an artist. Long hours, uncertain conditions, working within individuals' deadlines are all par for the course when you work for yourself.

Lenni's garage is his studio and to step into it is to be surrounded with his work. True

Lenni Schwarz - aka Krazy Kolors - is an artist who can do it all. From the goldleaf and stripe job seen on this display tank, to almost any kind of graphics imaginable, and complete paint jobs.

Lenni visualizes a design, draws it onto a masking film and begins to cut it prior to affixing to the tank.

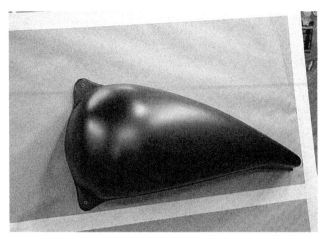

The tank has been painted Black and Cobalt Blue Kandi.

flames,signage, pinstriping, drawings, lettering, air-brushed creatures and characters… it's all too much for the average Joe to take in! And that isn't inclusive of the current job at hand. Once you've settled yourself with the surroundings you discover his creative juices are being stirred and he's contemplating his next move with the brush. Not a moment goes by where he's not thinking into the future, visualizing the next step. On this particular day Lenni was preparing for our photo shoot with a sample tank he'll use as a display for tradeshows and such. Well known for his graphic work on Donnie Smith's custom motorcycles, don't be surprised to see the tank at the next annual Donnie Smith Custom Motorcycle show held in St. Paul, Minnesota.

    With all of the gold leafing equipment ready to start it was obvious to see Lenni's skills and manner would once again take us on an easy to follow journey of his step-by-step process. Surface guilding, as it is properly referred to, is a technique new to many yet has been around for quite some time. The guilding, or leafing, can be done with silver, gold or a variegated gold. It is primarily used as an accent to enhance the overall look of the design. As you'll be able to see while you follow along, Lenni will also use his talents with air-brushing <u>and</u> pinstriping to give his design a refined and finished look. As in the past, Lenni's work here is done with precision and patience, which results in such quality work that anyone would be proud to display.

Lenni is able to be precise with his cuts by using an Xacto blade

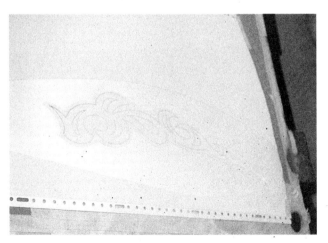

Leaving about ½ inch around the design the excess masking is removed so that it will lie down more smoothly on the curved surface.

7

Transfer paper is placed on top of the mask and the entire design is cut out. The back is peeled of its protective layer and adhered in position.

For an added flare he mixes one part HOK SG150 intercoat Pearl & flake Karrier, one part thinner, with a dash of Sapphire Kameleon Pearl.

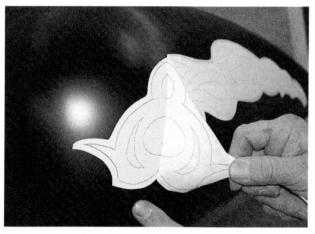

After any bubbles are removed with a small squeegee it becomes time to remove the transfer paper.

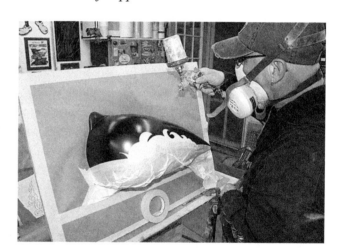

Two coats of intercoat clear are applied.

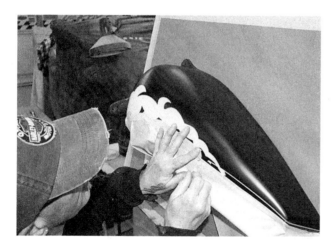

Lenni takes care to mask the bottom half of the tank with ¾ inch painters tape and paper mask to keep paint from entering the bottom half of the tank.

Only the top half will carry the Pearl.... a subtle element to the design.

Shadows are airbrushed using black.

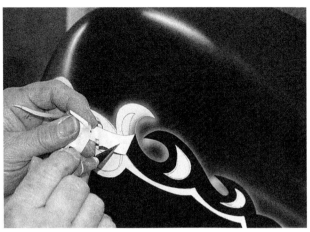

Using his Xacto knife he will gently peel off part of the mask.

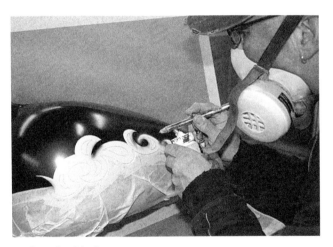

White highlights are next.

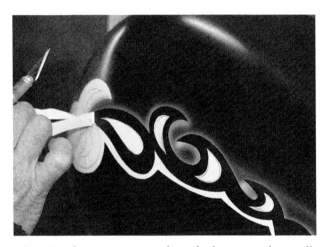

Care is taken so as not to disturb the pieces that will remain for now.

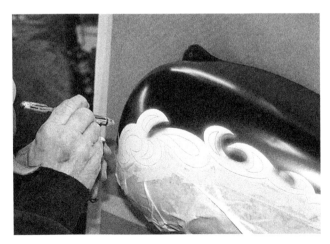

By adding shadows and highlights, Lenni has begun to create depth.

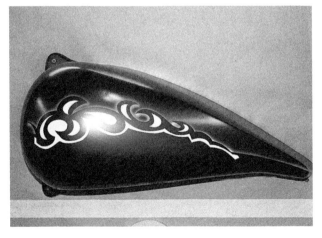

Notice how the shadows and highlights have now defined an outline to the design.

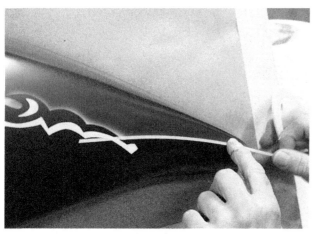

More masking is done by hand, flowing the design to the very edges of the tank.

More parts of the mask are removed and out of the way prior to the gold guilding, or leafing.

All the preparation is completed and the guilding process is ready to begin.

The metal leafing comes in sliver-thin sheets and can be purchased in different variations.

In order to penetrate the paint Lenni uses a bush to apply Paint Peniture- Fast Dry Gold Size to the areas that he intends to lay down his gold.

A piece of tissue paper separates the gold leaf allowing Lenni to pick up a sheet and gently place it over an area that was painted with the gold size.

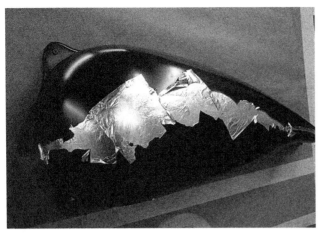

Lenni repeats this process until all of the Gold Size is covered with sheets of leafing. Usually the leafing remains on overnight.

A second round of Gold Size to penetrate the paint and Lenni is now in working in the enclosed spots of the design.

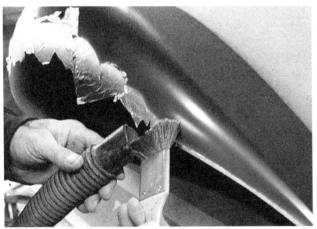

With this particular design Lenni is looking to achieve an aged look. So he will brush away any excess leafing after an hour of setting. His brush will leave very fine scratches and ultimately appear antique.

He has chosen a variegated leafing and he will again place sheets on the tank to cover all of the areas covered with Gold Size that has grown tacky.

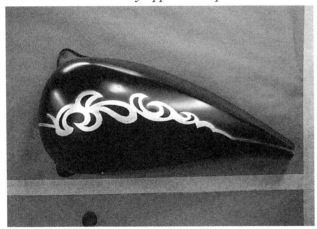

Any fine bits are vacuumed away and you can now see the design starting to take shape.

Using the side of your hand is a gentle, but firm way of patting down the leafing, releasing any bubbles and creating a bond.

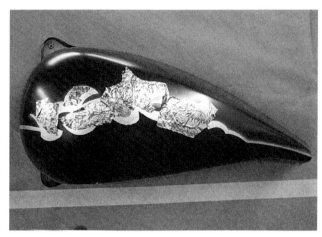

This leafing will sit overnight to bond into the paint.

A soft brush with a soft touch will eliminate any extra leafing. Keeping small flakes in control can be difficult, but by using a vacuum during the process you can eliminate most of the mess.

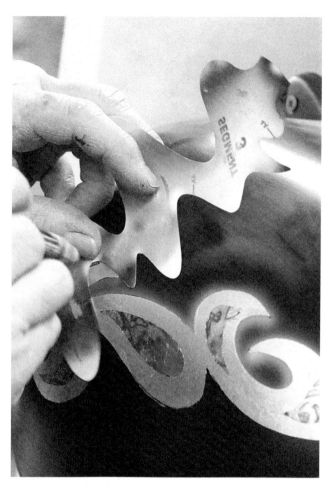

Lenni picks up his airbrush and begins to use a shadowing technique to create a beveled look. He has mixed red, brown and yellow to get a rust color he is happy with.

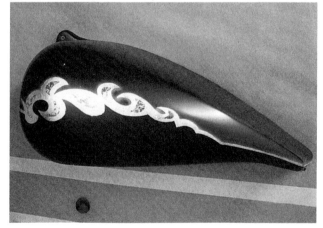

The 2 types of leafing have adhered and cheesecloth is used to wipe away any gold dust particles.

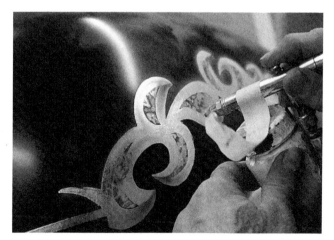

Highlights are added with white to really add dimension.

Lenni Schwartz Q&A

How long have you been painting?

Hard to believe, but over 30 years! It's amazing and certainly doesn't feel like that long. I've been able to create many different pieces of art throughout the years.

What type of art initially captured your passion?

For art class I found I really enjoyed drawing and painting in school. Even when I wasn't in art class my classroom papers had more art drawn on them than anything else! By high school I was painting backdrops for prom. About the same time I began painting trucks with my brother for our parents excavating business. This lead to doing the lettering on the trucks. In my spare time I would sit in the stands of sprint car races and draw the cars. I never kept any of the drawings I would always give them away!

How did you learn goldleafing?

Back in the '70s I saw some gold leafing on street rods. It was such an impressive look I just

had to try it. I located a book and read up on how to do it. I decided to buy a kit at a hobby store and began to experiment. It was all self taught. The first job I had leafing was the word "Ford" on the tailgate of a 1951 pickup.

Tell us about the types of painting you do?

Throughout the years I've taken on many different jobs, nothing is typical. I've learned to be diverse by airbrushing, pinstriping, lettering, acrylics on canvas or other objects that may come into the shop. I'll take on any challenge from the biggest being airplanes to the smallest little Hot Wheels cars!

What do you prefer to use for paint?

I typically use House of Kolor for airbrushing and pinstriping. I will also use One Shot or PPG for striping. If I'm painting a project with acrylics I prefer Liquitex out of the tube.

How about your preference for brushes?

When I'm striping I like to use Macks. Raphaels (which they don't make anymore) are also a favorite of mine. And typically for airbrushing I use an Iwata Eclipse, although I also like a Daashe or a Badger.

Where do you get your ideas, your inspiration?

I tend to be very observant of the environment I live in. Whether it's nature or man-made, I'm always absorbing shapes, colors, perspectives and trends. The library has always been a good source for books and magazines, and today the internet has just about anything you need to reference.

Do you have any advise for someone just starting out?

Be patient with yourself and it will come. It takes practice, practice and more practice!

Lenni will also go in with black in order to airbrush some darker shadows.

With more work to be done, Lenni uses a thin green masking tape used for painting. This will become his guide for pinstriping.

Here you can really see the dimension he has added with airbrushing.

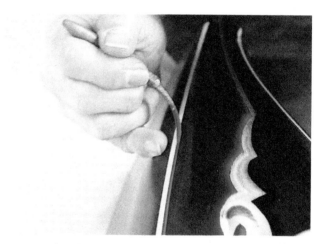

House of Kolor pinstripe paint is Lenni's choice of paint, and he begins with Lavender.

After the leafing is burnished - to appear antique - SG100 intercoat clear is applied to protect the work.

After he's used the guide it is removed and he proceeds to freehand.

*Continuing with Lavender he runs a line about ¼"
inch outside of the leafing.*

*The striping gives it a well-deserved personality by
keeping the lines small as to accent.*

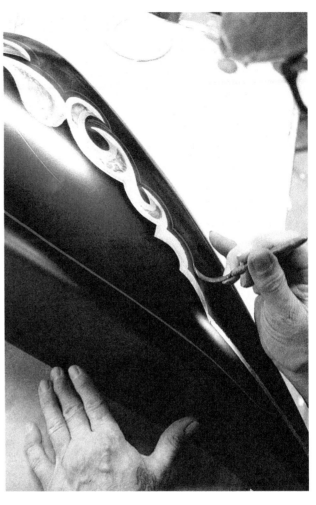

*If you do make a mistake with a stripe, use a combi-
nation of mineral spirits and wax grease lightly until
it's removed.*

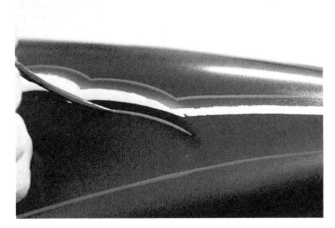

*Lenni must be sure-handed and very patient as there
is no room for errors.*

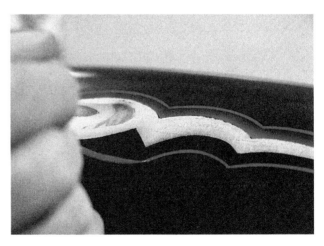

*Difficult to master, he will end all tips so they meet
smoothly.*

Using a mix of imitation gold and tan, Lenni stripes the top of the graphic.

... or it will end up transparent.

Remember not to over-thin the paint...

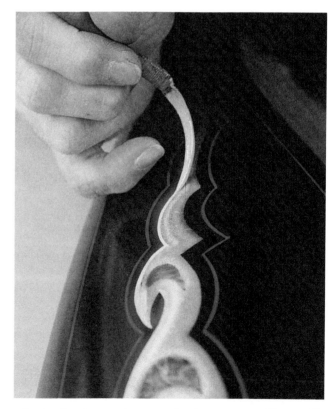

Again, having patience and taking time will pay off.

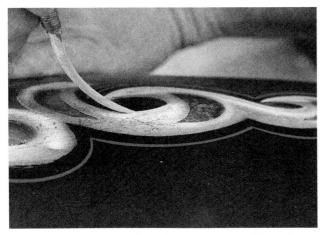

Another color is mixed with Imitation Gold and Brindle Brown.

A well-lit workspace will eliminate any shadows that may through you off.

He will continue the striping with a darker kolor at the bottom of the graphic to give it a heavier feel.

This will also allow you to see all the distant lines are clean.

Being careful not to rub his hand or finger through the other stripes, Lenni avoids smearing his work.

To create a clean and finished look, continue with the darker line over the lighter line by about 1/8 inch.

Lenni continues a smooth clean line…

After striping, 2 coats of SG100 are sprayed to seal it. Now a mixture of Crème kolor is used to airbrush striping blends.

…and he always works inward from point to center.

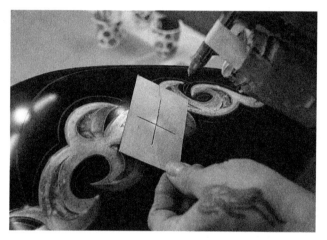

Highlight stars are sprayed using white to give it an extra illusion of shine.

Now that the lining is done, Lenni will check for any missed curves or lines. This is the time to correct or add kolor.

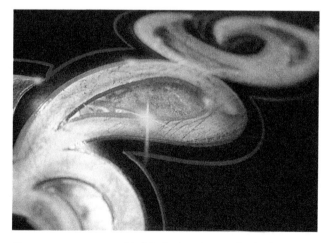

Be sure not to over highlight or it may look cluttered.

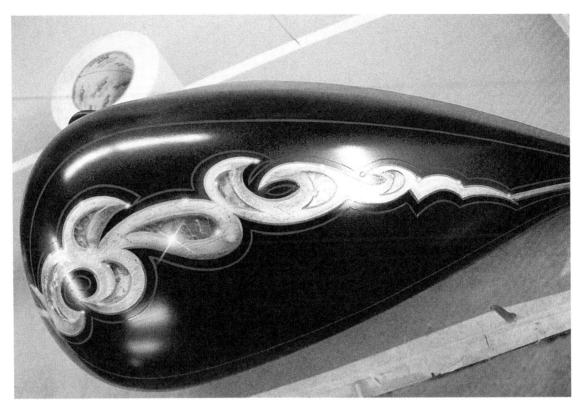

Now that he's at this point Lenni reviews the entire graphic to make sure nothing has been forgotten or that a blemish has not appeared. If any problems do arise, now is the time he'll fix it.

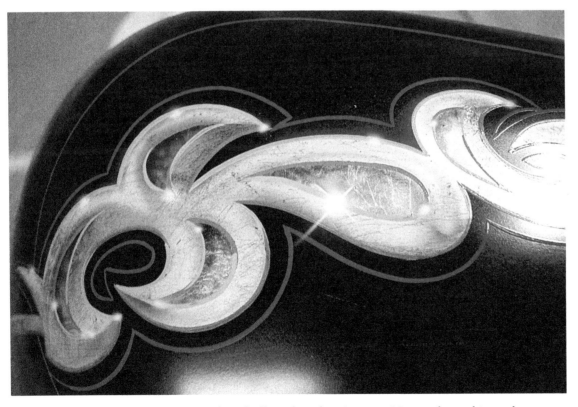

One coat of HOK SG100 is sprayed and allowed to dry. A gray 3M scratchy pad is used to lightly scuff and the result is truly impressive!

Story and photos by Deb Shade

Chapter Two

Kelley St. Croix-Bush Pin-Up

A Pin-up To Go Under

Upon walking into Kelley's shop you instantly feel nostalgia in the air. The building itself is made of brick, obviously many years ago, and served as the local auto service station in a very small community in rural Wisconsin. What remains with the structure provides a garage door, a supported engine lift, and exhaust fans in the paint area. All of this for Kelley's studio? Well not all of it. She shares her space with her husband, Bruce Bush. His forte is restoring old automobiles. Along with being a body man Bruce paints as well. In fact Kelley had been going to school for automotive

A pin-up with a certain island flavor by Kelly graces the underhood of her husband, Bruce's, Chevy hot rod.

bodywork and began her internship at Wizard Custom Studios. One thing led to another and now the two of them work side-by-side everyday, complimenting each other's work. They certainly don't limit their talents to automobiles, as both have motorcycles and tend to gain jobs in that industry too. The shop's name has also merged and become Wizard Custom Studios and St. Croix Airbrushing. After this sequence was photographed Kelley and Bruce have since moved into a new building which offers Kelley a gallery for her work.

When Kelley was approached to paint for this book, it gave her an excuse to finally focus on Bruce's '56 Chevy. He had asked Kelley to paint a pin-up inside the hood. Bruce has an admirable engine that he has painted to be one of a kind. When he shows the car, raises the hood, not only will the engine take your breath away, but there she'll be...a beautiful, nostalgic pin-up girl!

With an idea of what the pin-up would look like, Kelley went to work sketching. She measured the area under the hood and decided her piece would have to be approximately 24 inches high. Large paper, a pencil and eraser would be the tools she needed to create the first step in which would be a long and intricate process. Without a reference or photo to follow, Kelley's mental vision would flow down through her arm, her hand, and onto the paper to become a graphic woman of yesteryear.

Kelley is using a mixture of PPG paint and her SATA spray gun for the base of the skin.

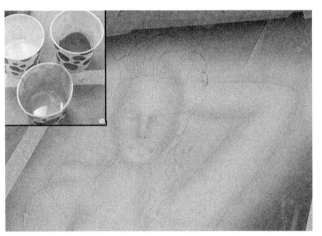

In order to create shade, a finer spray is required with an airbrush. Outlining the edges with a slightly darker tone will begin the process of shading.

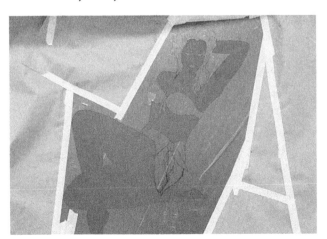

The hood has been painted with H of K basecoat clearcoat. A permanent marker is used to draw on frisket that she placed, and an Xacto knife works to cut out the first area to be painted, the skin.

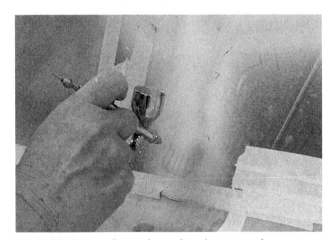

In addition to the outline, detail is created, as seen here with the toes.

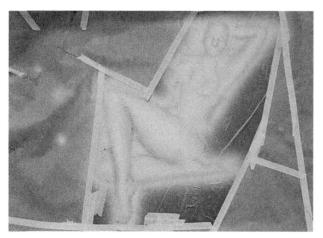

As you can see some of the detail is starting to take shape.

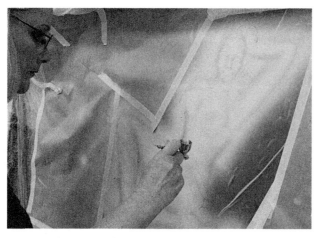

Using cream, tan, and root beer, 3 shades are mixed and sprayed to create depth in the shading process.

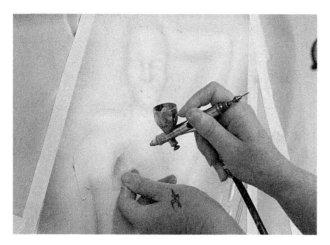

Kelley has cut a stencil to get a hard edge.

To shade in around the eyes, nose, and cheeks being precise is a slow process. Keep in mind when blending flesh tones that colors can change as the paint dries.

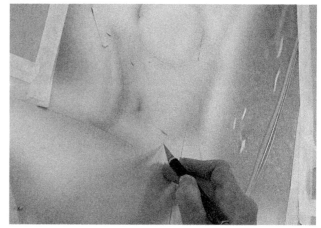

The next area to focus on will be the bathing suit. An Xacto knife will cut out the masked area to expose the suit.

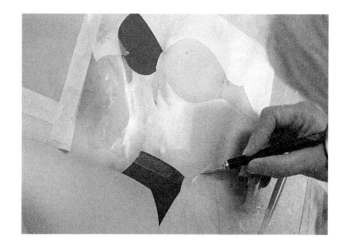

Special care is taken so as not to cut into the paint. Learning to get the proper amount of pressure with the knife requires practice and patience.

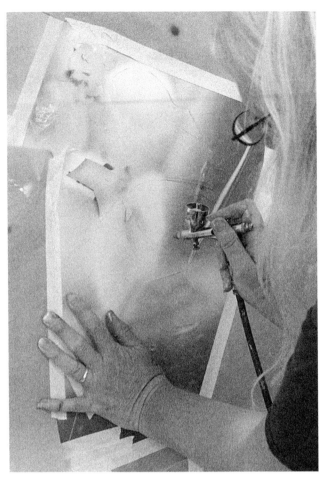

After masking off the body, the basecoat for the suit is sprayed with white. A dash of purple is then mixed in with the white to use for slight shadowing.

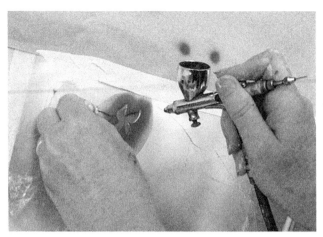

Each flower must be allowed to dry in between so as not to smear any of the red onto the white base.

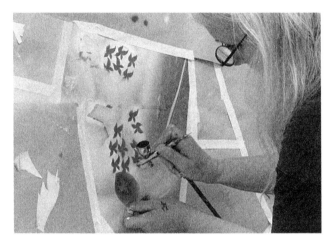

A darker, deeper red is used to shade in each stencil.

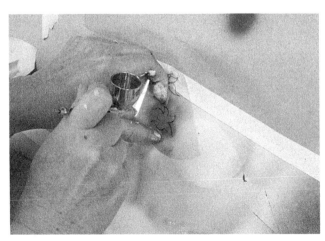

Kelley has cut a flower stencil to be used on the swim-suit. A red is custom mixed especially for the floral pattern.

Staying true to what the fabric would look like, Kelley turns the stencil as she works.

23

One piece of the frisket is removed at a time in order to work with the stencil, painting the flowers as if they are hiding beneath another piece of fabric in her suit. This can become tricky with fabric folds.

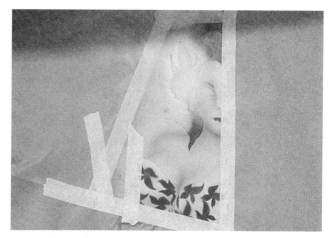

Everything else has been masked off and the flower is sprayed with white for the base.

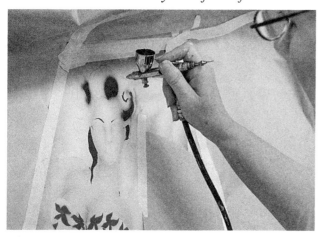

The face is masked off, yet the hair and eyebrows are cut out. With all other colors chosen prior to beginning, the color of the hair is something Kelley chooses at the time she is painting.

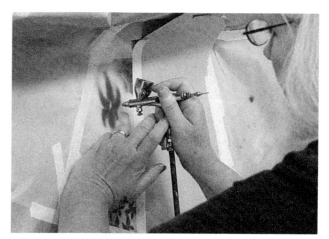

For the petals Kelley has chosen House of Kolor Red Pearl Shimrin to blend around the white.

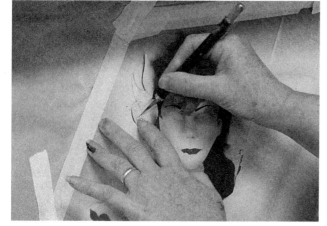

A Hibiscus flower is cut out afterward because it lies on top of the pin-up's hair.

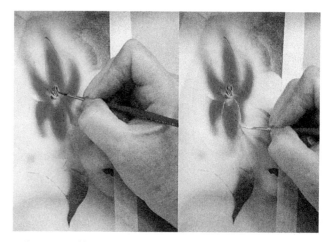

Chrome Yellow is the choice for the middle of the flower. The finer details are painted with a small brush, dots in the middle and the veins of the leaves.

Kelley St. Croix-Bush, Q&A

How long have you been an airbrush artist?

I've been airbrushing for 16 years, but my love for art began with my father. An engineer by day, his passion was oil painting. Seeing his work was inspiring! It wasn't until Jr. High that I became more involved on my own. My teacher, Mr. Nissen, took some of us kids under his wings. He was the type to see outside the box and recognize the importance of us having an outlet, a path to stay out of trouble. He would let us stay after school to work on projects and to my surprise he began putting my art in art shows. Teachers can definitely be influential in people's lives.

Tell us about the other painting you do, and the typical jobs that come through the shop?

I do wall murals, portraits, and of course pin-ups. I used to paint glass for churches, restoration of windows that were so old the original artist had long passed. It was an honor to keep their work alive. I painted Jesus along with several other biblical figures.

Where do you get your ideas?

I always seem to have an abundance of ideas in my mind, and not always the time to get around to all of them.

Who or what inspires you?

My inspiration began back in the '70s when I saw a motorcycle that was painted so beautifully. I spoke to the owner of the bike for quite a while, not realizing until years later that he was the artist! The beauty of his bike inspired me to pick up an airbrush and still today Jerry Snyder is someone I look up to.

What do you like for an airbrush?

Iwata HP or Micron, SATA for larger areas.

What paints do you typically use?

With automotive paints I use House of Kolor and PPG. When I really want to get bright, vivid colors to pop I'll use House of Kolor. I also like the pearls they have.

How do you reduce your paint? Do you over-reduce?

I use the automotive reducer that matches the brand, House of Kolor mostly. I do not over-reduce.

How much do you use the computer?

Computers aren't a part of my world, I prefer it that way.

Advise for anyone just starting out with an airbrush?

Try not to get frustrated, just stick with it. Do your best not to compare yourself to other artists and you'll find your own style!

In order to protect the flower frisket is placed over it.

Both irises are cut out and painted green.

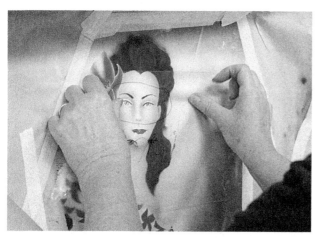

Kelley draws both iris and eyeliner on a separate piece of frisket…

Another color, blue, is sprayed to give dimension to the iris.

…this allows her to place the eyes where they look best, moving it about if necessary.

Care is taken to remove the masking and any mistakes made by cutting can be fixed by outlining the iris with a brush.

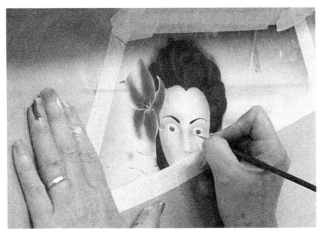

The inner corners of the eye are hand painted a very soft pink.

Continuing with black, the eyelids are lined.

Here you can see how Kelley has used the pink to gain detail.

The eyelashes are painted with a steady hand, the eyes have now come to life.

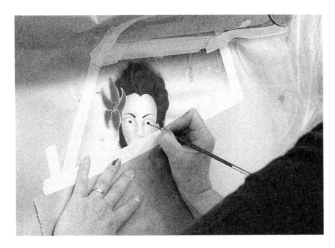

The pupils are now painted using black.

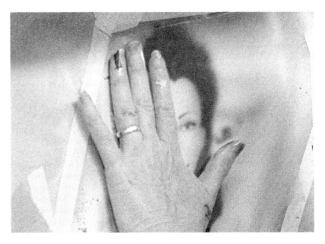

With the eyes done, the face is covered with frisket once again in preparation for the lips.

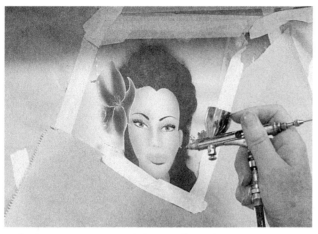

The lips are cut out of the mask and pink is sprayed as a base.

A white dot is also placed in the middle of each flower.

A fine brush is used to apply details to the lips. Brown is mixed with pink for shadowing and white is used to highlight.

Continuing to detail, Kelley outlines all of the flowers on the swimsuit with white.

All of the outline work gives the swimsuit a finished look.

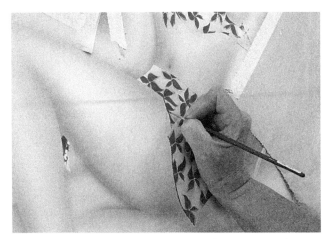

More fine detail is added to the fabric with red…a small fringe at the bottom of the suit.

Small strands framing the face are included.

Kelley makes a very fine outline to the suit…just enough to separate the white from the light tone of the skin.

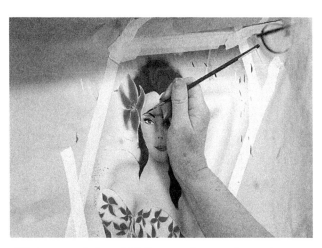

With a steady hand Kelley touches up the eyebrows.

Streaks in the hair are added and the hairline is defined. Several different shades of brown and red are swept throughout.

The lips also get touched up and darkened.

29

Kelley cuts out the top of the swimsuit in order to add shadows.

The pin-up appears to be finished, yet Kelley is not settled with the lack of definition between the swimsuit fabric and the skin tone. In order to create more of a contrast she decides to add more shading to the suit using Purple Passion.

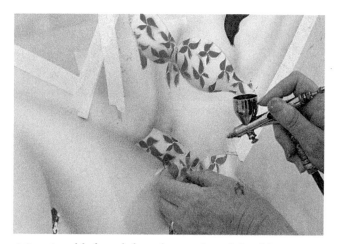

More is added to define the overlay of the fabric.

Masking off everything except the tie in the suit, shadowing is added.

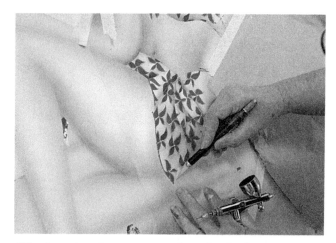

The last piece is cut to complete the shading.

All masking is removed and it's time to appreciate the pin-up. Kelley's husband, Bruce, will protect the artwork by spraying a coat of House of Kolor clear. The hood is then mounted on Bruce's '56 Chevy and it's ready for the show!

Story and photos by Deb Shade

Chapter Three

Dave Letterfly

Ford Trucks and Harley-Davidsons

When it comes to Davey Letterfly, the phrase old hippie comes to mind. It's not just the pony tail, it's more a matter of demeanor. Davey is gentle, direct and kind. The only thing he enjoys more than pinstriping a Harley Bagger or Ford pickup truck is traveling to the event where he can exercise his considerable artistic talents. When you pull into his yard in Florida, you will see not only the big motorhome that he uses to travel his "circuit" of mostly motorcycle shops in the winter, but at least one Volkswagen Vanagon (he owns at least three) that he tows behind the big rig.

This old school style of pinstripe design is built one inspiration at a time.

For Davey, what started as a childhood propensity to draw soon morphed into an apprenticeship in the sign industry. Pinstriping was only a very short step away. Today, he retains those skills learned in the sign painting shop. The careful layout, the ease with which he creates a balanced composition, the ability to work with brushes of almost any size to quickly create designs that simply work - without elaborate masking and stencils - all are skills and abilities learned as a sign painter. Which is not to say that Dave can't use an airbrush. For many years he made a living painting elaborate scenes on huge motorhomes with his airbrush.

Today, Dave spends a lot of time doing pinstriping for bikers - a clientele who not only insist on personalizing their two-wheeled vehicles, but who also appreciate art done by hand. From event to event and dealership to dealership, Dave and his side-kick Mike (and one large labrador) make their way across the country, leaving behind a large group of smiling customers.

A writer as well as a painter, Dave does a regular newsletter: Tales of a Traveling Airbrush, which he sends in print or e-form to anyone on his mailing list. Topics include everything from the joys of travel to the people he meets along the way, as well as the promotional information you would expect.

Mike uses a technique to clean the surface learned from the Karate Kid.

The design starts in the center of the tailgate with a simple shape.

Sharp points are the result of strokes that terminate together.

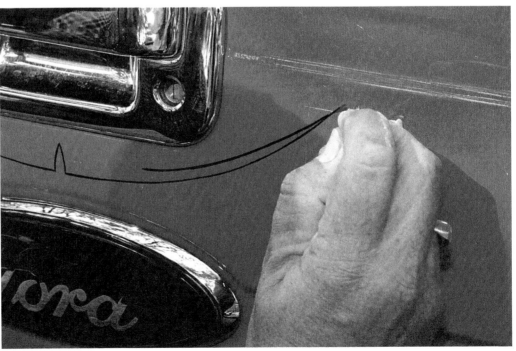

33

Wide angles are more manageable when both strokes begin there.

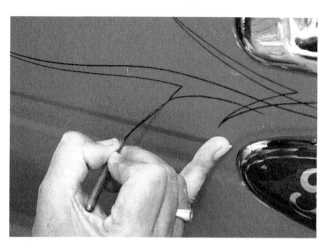

Consistant width strokes are the touchstone of an accomplished pinstripe artist.

Design influence comes from seeking a pleasant manner to begin and end each line.

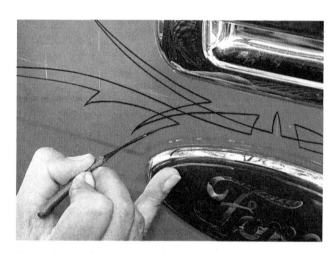

Like the rhythms of a melody the design contains repeated features.

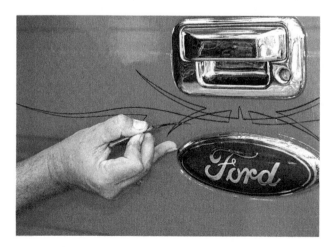

Each motif decision is made one at a time.

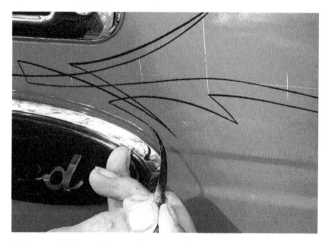

The anchoring line relates to the oval the design will compliment.

Underneath the oval the strategy is repeated.

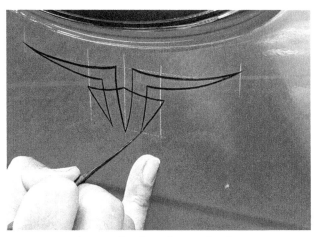

Knowing when to finish is the result of striping wisdom.

Beginning and ending decisions facilitate evolution of design.

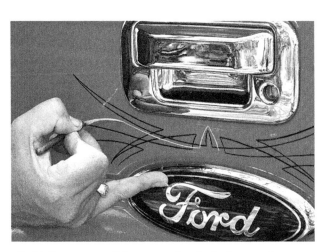

Gold lines are striking over the dark that makes up the background.

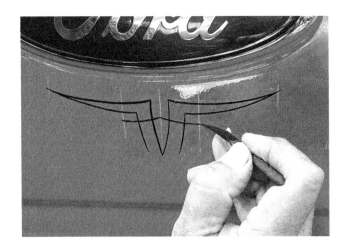

Parallel lines create a complimentary rhythm.

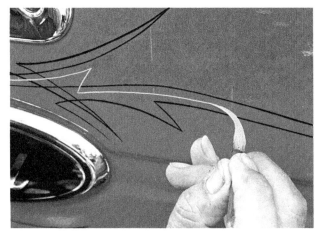

Pathways for the new color are apparent throughout the design.

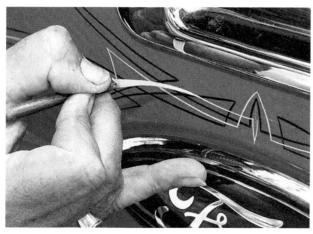

Delicate features add detail designed to create awe in the viewer.

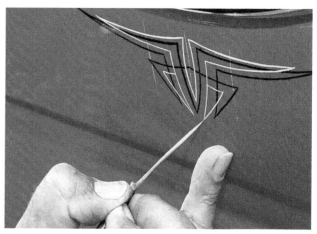

The classic simplicity of intrigue is accomplished with precision.

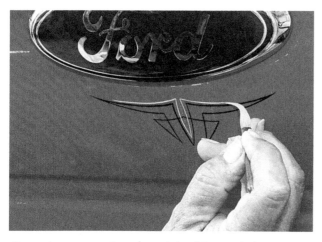

Sometimes repeating the original intent is best.

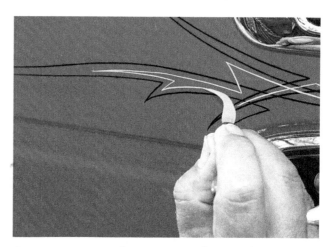

Inspiration comes from existing elements here.

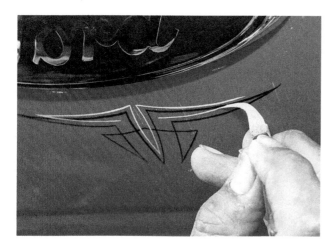

The re-run is enjoyed more places than just on television.

Like an electric circuit the final span completes the energy transfer.

The tip is all that touches the truck leaving a thin line of paint.

I set the brush down - and the stroke begins with a blunt end.

Rhythm is introduced with interest throughout the area being decorated.

After a short line, a long graceful stroke creates intrigue.

Over the centerline, criss-crossing creates an opportunity for another shape.

I put a long diamond in the center of the design.

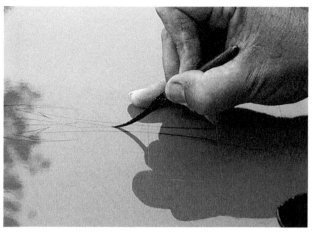

Leaving a sharp point at the end of the stroke is easy to do with this brush.

A good line is the result of ideal paint viscosity, a great brush and being dialed in.

Finishing two long strokes into a sharp point is a practical way to use this brush.

Repeating the strategy of starting a stroke with a blunt end and finishing with a sharp point.

With a motif made of all vertical lines, a laterial one really adds interest.

Allows the motif to enjoy a consistant tempo.

Keeping the design size manageable means I can bridge over the wet paint.

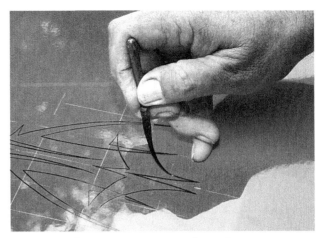

Inverting the stratagem seems a logical way to continue.

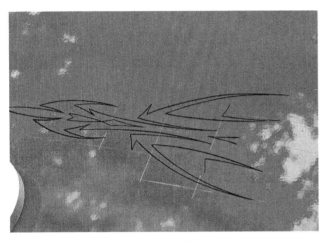

The rhythm of the few lateral lines is apparent here.

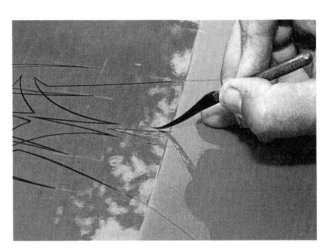

Intricate features provide contrast to the whole.

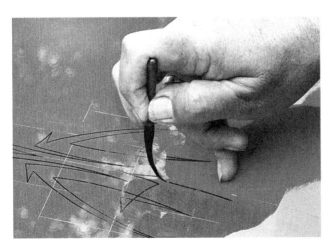

Sharp points that aim up are created the same way as the rest.

A central axis for the foundation of the design is created the same way.

Dave "Letterfly" Knoderer

I started painting as a kid. My mother noticed I had a gift so she encouraged me with sketchbooks and art workshops for children. After high school, I played drums with the circus and learned how to travel. Circus people find out what you do best and pretty soon I was decorating the trucks. There was an old man there, a sign painter who taught me the basics of his trade.

I apprenticed in the sign trade in 1976 while working at two shops. I became good with the brush, learned the alphabets (I needed five), and how to scale-up to any size using a yardstick. I also learned composition and layout skills, and the work discipline of the journeyman. It was a good place to learn closely guarded secrets.

When the computer began to take over the sign trade, I discovered a huge market airbrushing murals on the backs of motor homes. That morphed into mural painting the interiors of the new Harley-Davidson dealerships - and being around the bikers introduced me to the next chapter of my creative career; being a traveling motorcycle artist.

What is your favorite brush and why?

Brushes and the work I do have changed. As the years go by the brushes I use get smaller and smaller as I do finer work. My favorite pinstripe brush is the Mack series 10. I like the length of the Series 10, I use the shorter Xcaliber but only when it's windy. Grey quills, outliners, the "Virus," economical filberts, brights and flats are in my arsenal.

Do you ever modify the brushes?

With a new pinstripe brush, I first look to see how it's put together. Each one is assembled by hand so each is unique. There are subtle differences from one to the other. When they're new, most of them require a trim to get the right amount of hair in the right proportion at the tip where you do the work. Typically I trim with a razor blade to get exactly the brush I want.

Which paint do you use?

Mostly One-Shot. I miss the old time One-Shot, heavy with lead. The formula now is different; the black doesn't work as well as it used to. I use Ronan black now, and One-Shot for the rest. One-Shot did improve the silver, now much better than years ago.

Do you ever bury the pinstripes and brush-painted artwork under clear?

Sometimes. When I do I put clear over my paint with good success. The trouble is, dry One-Shot is semi porous and if urethane solvent soaks in the One-Shot will expand and wrinkle. The secret is to build up an insulating layer of dry urethane first. I put on three dust-coats, letting each

Dave "Letterfly" Knoderer

dry before putting on the next. Those three thin coats make an insulating layer between the One-Shot and the hot solvents in the final, wet coat of urethane clear.

Do you have rules about your designs, or how many times a line can cross another line or about things getting too crowded?

I have a style and some unwritten rules. I don't want to have 3 lines intersect at the same place, or have a line intersect the corner of another line. I tend to make long circuits and then come back later and connect them. David Hightower is my hero, I really like his designs.

The Air Force logo and Vietnam service bar are more of Dave's work, done without stencils or airbrush.

Do you design on the fly?

Hey, are you making fun of me? First, I assess the shapes and lines of the project in front of me and seek to compliment what exists, then make design decisions while I'm working. You don't want all the lines to be identical. Like poetry, I seek an interesting rhythm. I just get started, allow inspiration to guide me and go. I don't have it drawn out ahead.

There are different styles of design; old school, loopy, cruising and touring bike styles. When I talk to a customer, I find out which style they like and create a new design on their bike using this information so the work is their own.

Do you layout a grid ahead of time?

I like to use a grid because I want the design to be accurate and symmetrical. Like on the top of a tank or fender, I use a grid as reference to ensure the design is precisely the same on both sides. I typically have a default way of beginning, with an incomplete teardrop. Part of what influences the design is how the brush works. It's easy to begin with a blunt line and have a point at the end. Elements of the design with sharp points occur at the end of brush strokes. I tend to connect the points of every brush stroke and make an unending, interwoven line for my design.

Tell us a little about your Custom Paint Workshops?

The workshops occur during the winter at my home in Florida. I teach the techniques of all the disciplines of the custom painter. The five-day seminar is divided into five categories with different criteria each day, enabling people to take just one day, or three or five. I cover Sign Painting, Lettering, Pinstriping, both Freehand and Frisket Style Airbrushing, Wet Blended Pictorial Painting, Gold Leaf and all aspects of Custom Paint. Also; for aspiring road warriors, strategies that the promoters at Sturgis and Daytona don't want you to know. On Saturday we have a panel jam party where established painters from the region rub elbows with the students.

The upstroke is another way to use this great brush.

Spontaneous grace connects the waiting elements.

Clean unions of lines are the result of care and precision.

The illusion of symmetry is the goal.

Using poetry tactic, the design begins to rhyme.

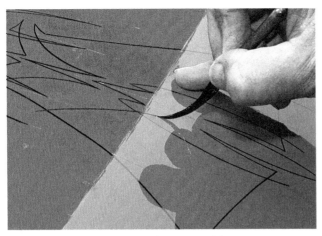

The span from orbiting elements adds continuity.

Flanks are not just for military strategy.

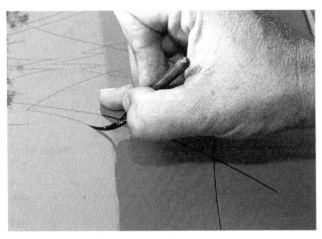

With so much wet paint, my choices now are influenced by where my pinkie can rest.

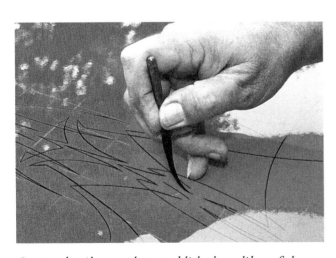

Precise details are what establish the calibre of the intention.

The lateral element seems to have all else orbiting around.

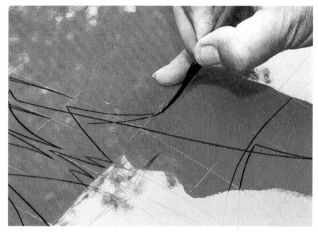

Over the longest line of all, an interruption adds rhythm.

New shapes result from overlapping elements.

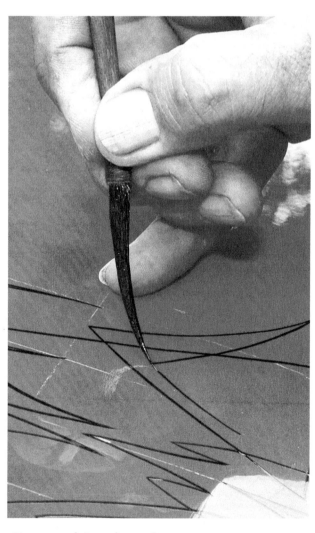

Extra tough is ending a line at a corner.

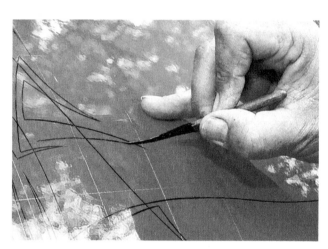

Graceful curves make the components of the design.

Radiating from a neighboring line, more rhythm is created.

Gold takes the spotlight in this color combination.

Finding opportunities is the whole idea.

New directions for individuals are found while the design is underway.

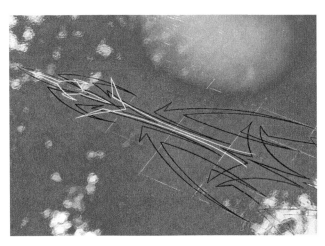

Connecting across the center establishes individual shapes.

This void now appears to have an intentional shape within.

A mass of parallel lines is always kool.

Up stroke into a point is another variation to include.

Note the short lateral and the mass of vertical - makes for good rhythm.

Thinking in terms of mixing up the kinds of features avoids monotony.

Repeat like a stanza and the design begins to resemble a melody.

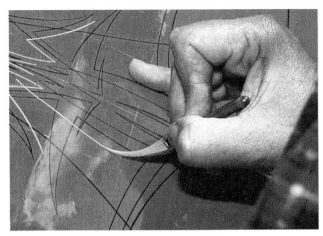

Getting the new color across the entire design takes perseverance.

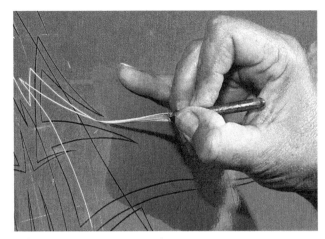

Shape points are spectacular.

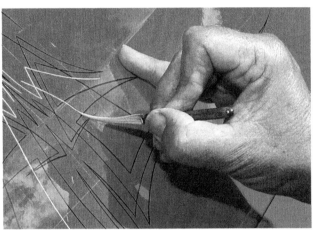

Long strokes compliment interesting deviation.

Small captured shapes qualify as staccato elements.

Starting at a point is challenging.

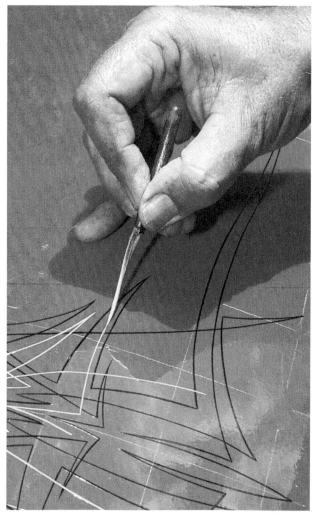

Compliment what is working with some flattering imitation.

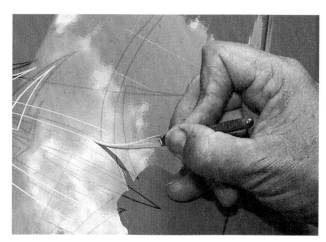

Strengthen the vertical chassis with yet more nice lines.

The foundation has an interesting collection of lateral inspirations.

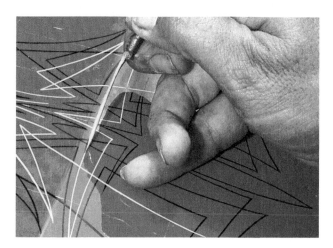

What was once an interesting void is now full of color.

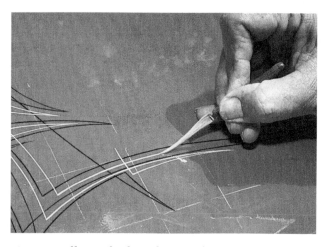

On a smaller scale the sideways elements repeat the flavor begun initially.

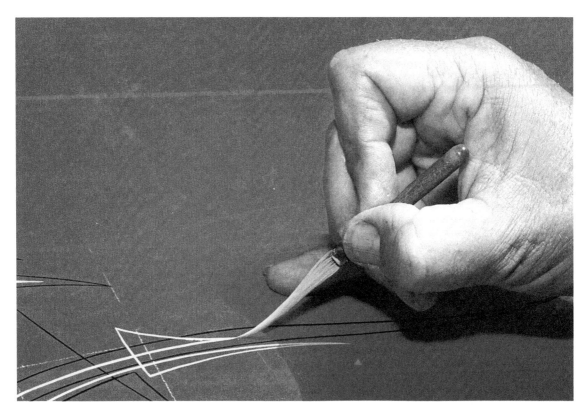

Bulk ending in graceful tips is yet another example of mixing interesting features.

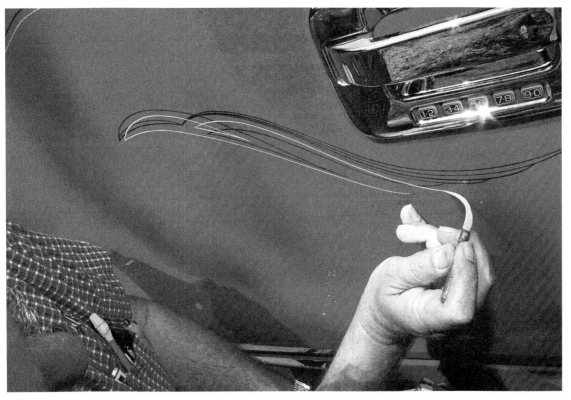

Don't forget graceful shapes to compliment the door hand.es.

Chapter Four

Leah Gall

More Complex Than Most

Leah Gall works out of an old barn that she shares with Brian, her body-man/custom painter husband and partner. The two of them make a good tag team, with Leah on the airbrush and Brian on the spray gun. Together, there aren't many custom paint projects they can't do.

Primarily self taught, Leah's early experiences include working at a T-shirt shop in Florida, and another in Sturgis, where she

The wicked cowgirl with the big six-shooter is Leah Gall's latest creation. Applied to a Bagger fairing, this very nice piece of art will be used as a display piece in their various booths.

worked in the Big Daddy Rat booth. Today, her work includes every imaginable airbrush design, applied to both custom motorcycles and four-wheeled hot rods.

Watching Leah is always interesting and insightful. She works without hesitation and mixes colors on the fly with an intuitive sense of where she's going - of how to get the perfect warm brown or soft yellow to compliment the rest of an in-progress design. There's always a nice flow, not only to the image itself, but to the process by which it's created.

Though she's no stranger to solvent-based paint, Leah has recently begun to use more of the waterborne materials from PPG. "I usually don't wear a mask," says Leah, "and I just don't like breathing the fumes, but the waterborne is different and it definitely does take some getting used to."

The project seen here is more complex than some, and took over three days to complete. Unlike some artists who use the computer as one of their essential tools, Leah often starts with a pencil sketch of her own, explaining as she does, "By the time I get it drawn out I know I like the image, and by cutting it apart I've created a whole series of stencils that I can use during the painting. And this way it's my image and not something I stole."

"I prefer using paper for my masks," explains Leah. "Sometimes I use Friskit, or transparent masking material, but the edges end up so sharp and harsh, I really like the paper masks better because the edges are always softer."

Anyone who wants to see Leah in action and find out how she creates images that seem to lift right off the surface need only sign up for one of her seminars, or look her up at the SEMA show where she toils away for SATA, the same company that created the signature Leah Gall spray gun.

Brian painted the fairing candy gold over metallic silver, and then added a coat of intercoat clear – "the clear helps me see the color as it will look after we apply the final clear," explains Leah.

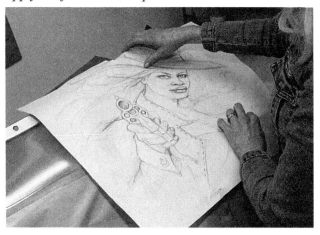

The drawing of the cowgirl is my own, I made the gun bigger so it would look closer to the viewer. I'm holding it to make sure the size is right and to see where I'm going to place it.

I use an Xacto knife to cut the drawing into major pieces - they become like a free hand stencils. I prefer paper because it leaves softer edges.

Now I've placed the pieces of the drawing on the fairing, and left gaps between, so a coat of color will give me an outline of each section.

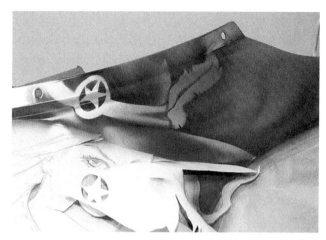

I'm using the translucent brown with the light background showing through. Gold is one color, brown is the other, it's a monochromatic picture right now.

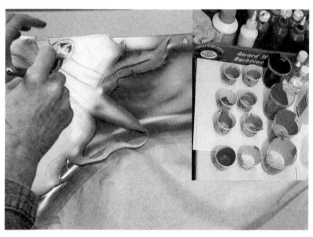

I created a transparent, darker golden brown that I'm using here - one of my pre-mixed colors from a palette that goes with the gold back ground.

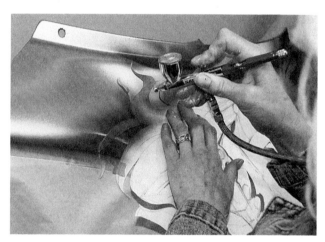

Holding a stencil by hand like this lets the air lift it on the edges so I don't get that hard edge.

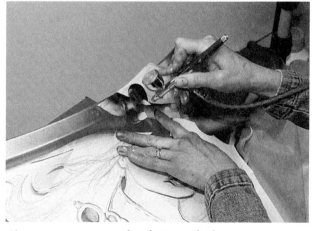

I'm starting to spray her hair with the same transparent brown, I will use this for lots of the work. At this point I'm working in light and dark, I like to let the lighter colors show through.

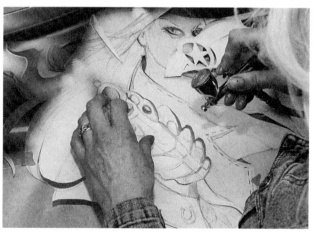

I'm creating outlines to see where everything is going to be. I continue doing this until I have most of the major pieces located correctly.

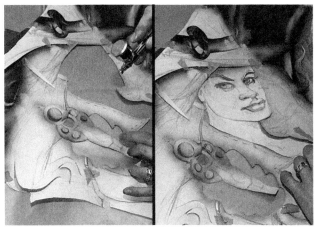

I've moved some stencils around to exposed some flesh, and I'm using a medium flesh tone to fill in those areas.

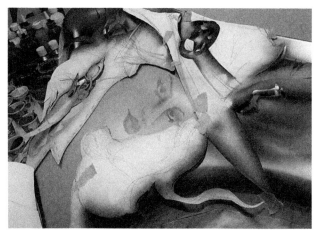

Take a look and check how this is progressing, the facial features are in place, some of these I did using small free-hand stencils.

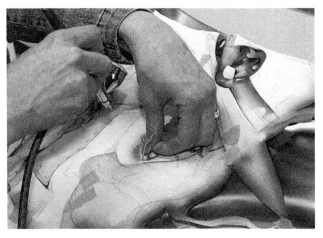

Next, I put the face stencil down. With a darker flesh tone and the cut outs…

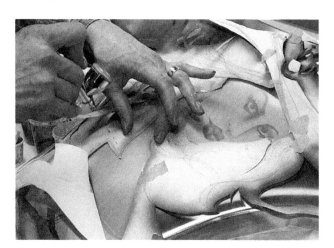

I'm spraying darker flesh tone here, where the flesh meets the clothes, to add dimension and depth.

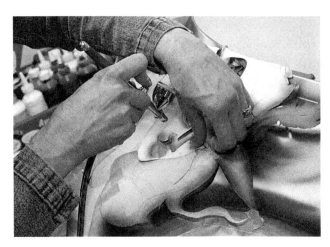

… I can layout her facial features.

I'm continuing to use the same flesh tone to shadow the area under her chin, and to enhance her breasts, she's gotta have cleavage.

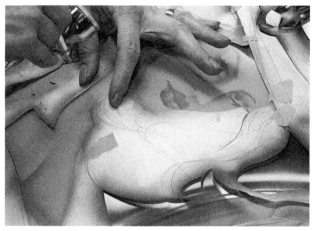

I've added a little darker color to my medium brown and continue to shape out her facial features and shadows.

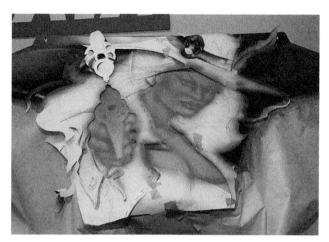

You can see I've continued to work and define the hands, the same as I did on face and cleavage.

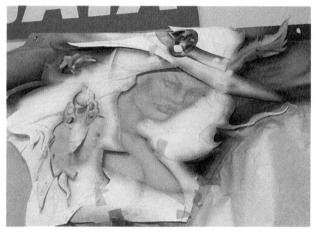

The light and dark areas help create that 3-D effect.

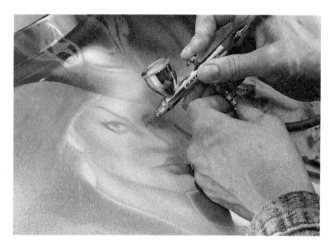

Working very close to the surface, I use dark brown to enhance the eye details.

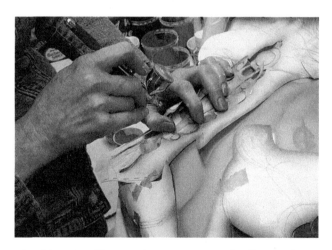

At this point I'm starting to separate the fingers from each other with a small slit between each one and a darker brown paint.

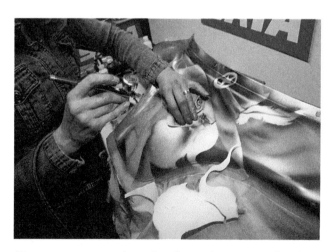

I'm starting to work on her hair, shaping out her locks using darker translucent brown and leaving as much gold showing through as possible.

I use the same color to work on the gun and her hand.

Progress shot, those lips need some work...

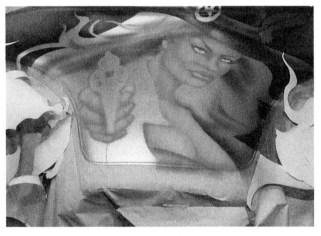

A progress shot. I've not completed the hair yet, note all the gold that's showing through.

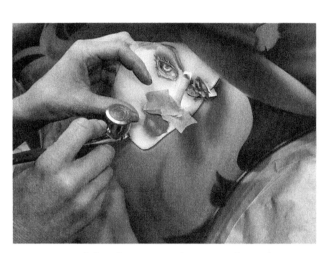

... I re-mask her lips to give her more lipstick...

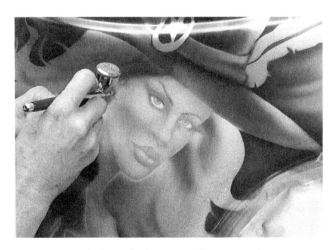

I'm using a lighter flesh tone to bring out her eyes and upper facial features. I call it going over her facial features to create more dimension.

... note the effect of the lipstick done with a translucent red. I want her to have pouty lips.

I'm working on hand details, using translucent material for a mask…

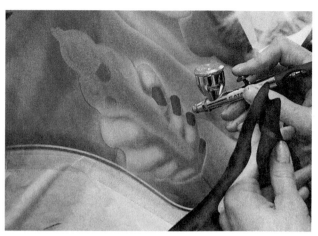

I spray in the red leaving some highlights showing through. I also used some brown to create shadows on the lower part of each fingernail.

… I've cut out each fingernail…

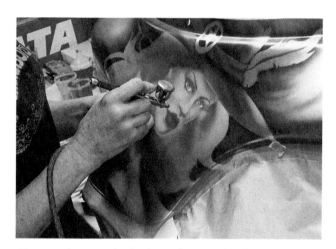

I'm not done with the lips, they need a few more dark details.

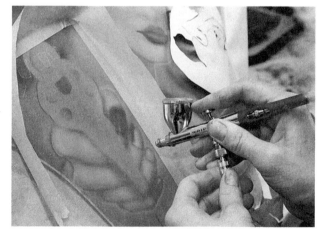

… and spray on the color, this is the same red I used on her lips.

I'm using a dark brown to darken the eyebrows and add eye details.

Leah Gall Q&A

How did you become an airbrush artist?

One of my first jobs as an artist was working a flea market in Florida, painting T-shirts. Later I worked at the Ron Jon Surf Shop and then booths in Daytona painting helmets. I also worked in Sturgis painting mostly T-shirts. And because of the time I spent in Daytona and Sturgis I was exposed to motorcycles, and started working on those too.

When I got together with Brian 23 years ago we really started to focus on motor vehicle work.

Tell us about some of the typical jobs that come through the shop?

We do lots of motorcycle work with skulls, fire and flames, patriotic themes or chicks. Between Brain and I we can do airbrushing, graphics and the overall paint job. So it's one stop shopping for the customer. We are not a high volume shop. We put heart and soul into each job.

Where do you get your ideas, who or what inspires you?

Everywhere. I have stacks and stacks of magazines, and all my drawings. I live in the country, surrounded by nature. When I do come up with an idea I try to make sure I filter it with my own mind and process it with my own hands so it is mine and mine only.

What do you like for an airbrush?

I use the SATAgraph 4 and their Dekor gun.

What paint(s) do you typically use?

I use any kind of paint I have to, I'm very versatile that way. I use automotive solvent-based paint, and I also like the waterborne paint.

How do you reduce your paint? Do you over-reduce?

I mix it so it works for me, it depends on the project. I just do it intuitively according to the detail I need to paint and the airbrush I'm using.

Other tricks you're learned along the way?

I let the background work for me, like I did with the job on the fairing. It takes time to learn, but a nice medium tone background will always help you out.

How much do you use the computer, can you give us an example?

When I'm designing for the client, I like to show them what the finished paint job will look like. Photoshop is a great tool for design, you can look at a concept in different colors. We also use the computer and plotter to cut some of our stencils and masks.

Advice for anyone just starting out with an airbrush?

Stuck to it, through highs and lows. It's not easy, but it will become easier. And practice your drawing skills so you can free hand with the airbrush. That way you aren't always tied to the stencils and masks.

Whatever you put your hand to, do it with all your might. Choose carefully the things you do and don't be afraid to say no sometimes. Have fun.

The brown I used for the eyes and eyebrows is also useful to darken the nostrils…

The same dark color used in the last panel can be used to add details to her hair.

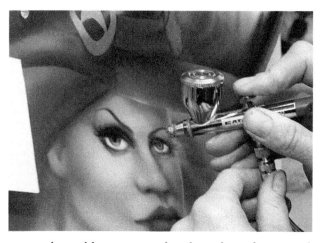

… and to add even more details to the eyebrows and eyes.

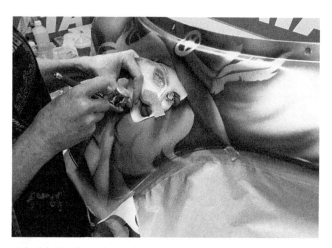

I hold the facial mask I place and use the darker brown under her chin, and to darken some of her hair.

I've Started on her hair, and touched up areas on the hat and under her chin.

You can see I've added swirls to her hair and lots more detail with the darker brown.

I'm using a hand-held mask and still working on hair details with the dark brown. It's important to let the golden background show through in select areas.

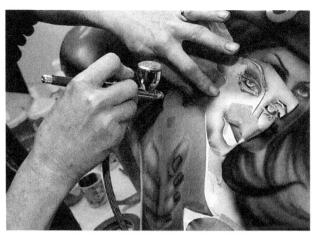

I'm holding a stencil free hand and add bright purple…

Progress shot, the face and hair are coming along, but the hand and gun need more work.

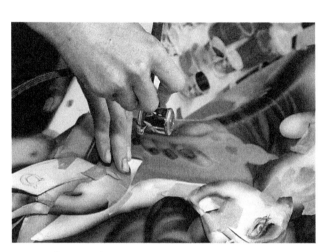

… to the trench coat.

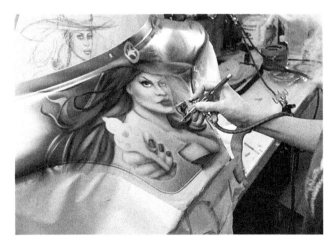

Using the airbrush free hand I continue to work on hair, hat and bodice with the darker brown.

The purple is really set off by the browns because it's on the opposite side of the color wheel.

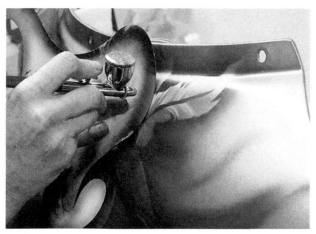

I'm using the same purple on the feather, with help from a hand-cut French curve.

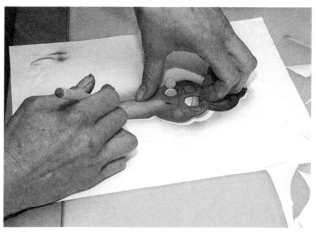

I lay my cutout of the gun from earlier on a blank sheet, and spray around it, to make another stencil...

A little bit of color really helps that feather stand out...

... which I lay on top of the transparent masking material I've already placed over the gun, and cut out the shape of the gun...

... I've used the same color on the brim of the hat. Also on her cheeks to bring some of that color down into her face.

... that you can see me lift off here, prior to painting the gun.

Before painting the gun I build a tent of masking tape to avoid getting any overspray on the rest of the painting.

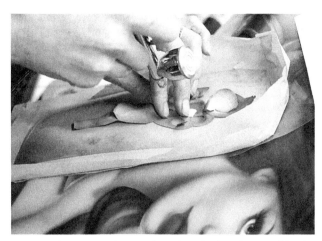

Using the original stencil and a darker brown/black I begin adding details to the gun.

I'm beginning to spray in what I call a dirty tan color.

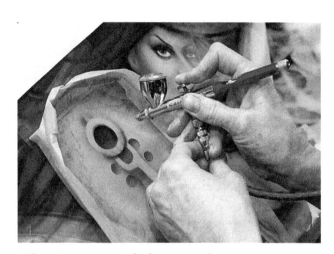

Then I come in with the same color…

And I've now covered the gun entirely.

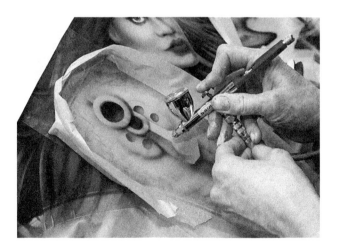

… and add more details without a stencil, working freehand.

It takes time and patience…

I've put down a piece of clear masking material, then cut out the area of the collar.

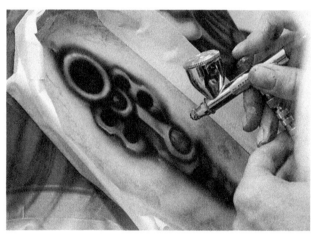

… until I've add enough details and color…

I like the PPG Envirobase paint, but you do have to run it through a filter before spraying it with the airbrush.

… that I'm happy with the gun.

In a multi-step process with and without the use of a paper mask, I add more of the violet-blue to the collar and other parts of her jacket.

Sometimes the only way to create really fine details is with a small brush.

... as you can see a piece of transfer paper makes this much easier.

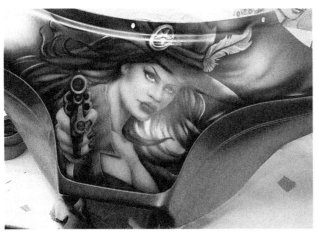

I'm done with the main image, now it's just a matter of adding some filigree and details to the lower panels.

I'm applying a buckskin color, using a SATA Dekor2000 trigger-style airbrush. I have to keep in mind that the background color will show through and is part of the design.

I place these stencils - cut out on the plotter - on the band that runs across the fairing...

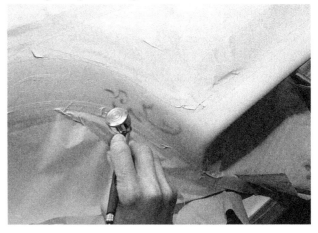

Next I take an opaque tan and use it to shadow around the filigrees.

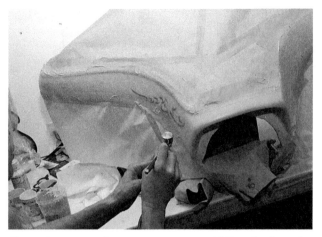

I continue spraying opaque tan until I've shadowed all the filigreed pieces and the upper tape line.

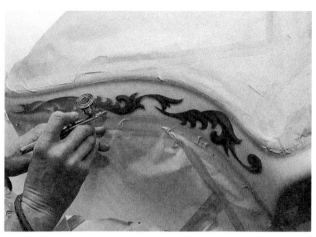

For some of this detail work it's easier to work free hand.

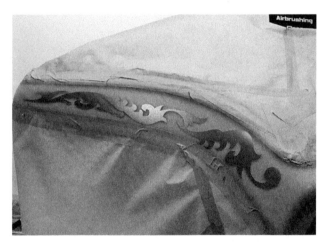

Progress shot shows our filigree of the original gold, after I've pulled stencils, before I add the details.

The finished filigree, shadowed and detailed in 3 steps: before the stencil was pulled, with a hand-cut stencil, and freehand.

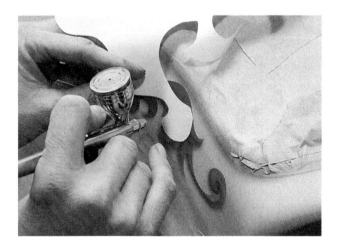

I cut out another French curve stencil and use it to add shadow and dimension to the filigrees.

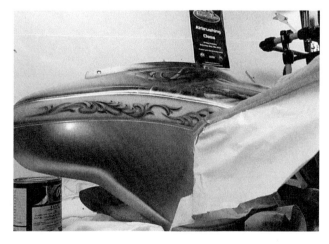

Now we pull all the masking off the fairing...

... and check out our work.

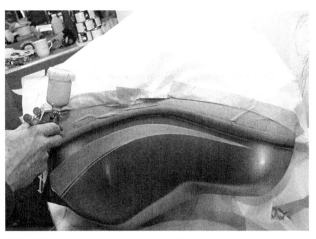

Now I use the Dekor from SATA to apply a dark brown to the edges of Brian's design.

Almost finished, Brian wants to add some detail to the fairing's lower panels and does a simple tape out.

After pulling the masking you see how much the simple design on the lower fairing added to the total design.

The finished art. This job was a lot of work, but could have been so much more work if we hadn't worked with a background color that shows through. Note how, with a few exceptions, all the colors are from the same color palette.

Chapter Five

Nub

A Bad Ass Paint Job

When someone's been on TV as much as Nub, you kind of expect him or her to be, if not arrogant, at least possessing of a certain amount of 'tude. Which is not the case with Nub. He is simply a talented guy with a certain amount of

luck (his description), and – at least for now – a lot of people who come to him for bad-ass paint jobs.

When you walk into his shop, a converted barn, the first thing you see on the floor is the

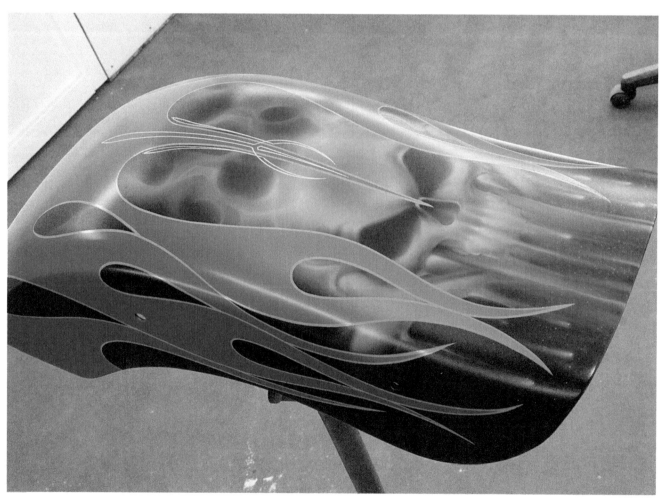

Truly a bad-ass and very creative skull and flames combo paint job from one of the world's best known custom painters.

bull dog Moe, asleep. The lower level is divided up into two small stalls, and one spray booth. Upstairs is a bit more interesting, with a music room/office on one end and one big multi purpose area that fills the rest of the upstairs.

In addition to a certain artistic talent, Mr. Nub has a wicked and twisted sense of humor. Side projects include T shirts with his own unique brand of monster, and stickies of aliens; again, not just any aliens, but rather his own unique brand of extraterrestrial visitor.

Though he once ran a commercial shop with four, full time painters, he let it all go. He also let go of the overhead and the stress of keeping five people working on multiple paint jobs. Today, Nub is very content to work alone in the converted barn a hundred feet from his house. The only painter in the barn now is a guy named Nub, assisted by two women who answer an endless string of emails, and ship monster shirts around the world.

Nub does the basecoat and airbrush painting, but no real body work and minimal preparation. When there's a fender with a dent, or a gas tank that the customer wants extended, it goes to a neighboring shop, run by one of Nub's friends, and comes back ready for the first coat of primer.

Though he's known for great designs implemented with the airbrush, there isn't much that Mr. Nub can't do. As seen in this chapter, he's just as handy with a pinstripe brush as he is with an airbrush. The pinstripes commonly compliment or complete the airbrush work, though sometimes the 'stripes are a full-blown design of their own.

Sometimes you find a guy doing exactly what he's supposed to do. A musician lost in perfect chords and progressions, a jeweler making rings from gold and silver. Nub is one of those. With plenty of work from appreciative customers and Moe for company, he's a man toiling away on his craft - toiling with a big smile on his face.

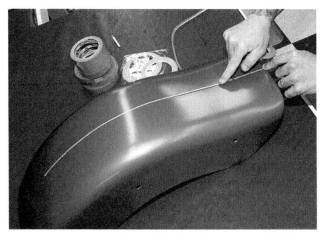

The tins are sprayed Kandy Blue basecoat and left to dry. I begin my layout with 1/8 inch tape down the middle to give me my center point.

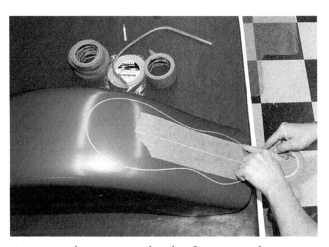

I use 2 inch tape on each side of my center line to give myself another reference point to help keep the flames even down the middle of the design.

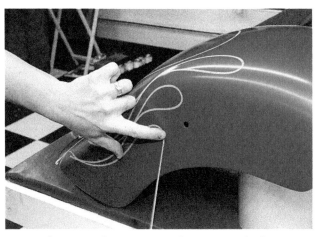

Once the center line is mapped out, I work the Flames towards the sides with the 1/8 inch tape.

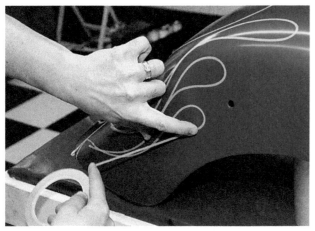

Using my right hand to steer the tape...

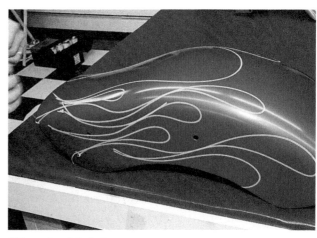

That should do it.

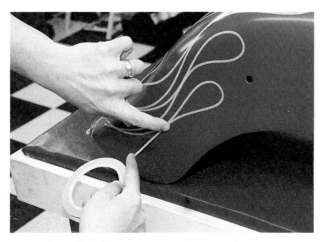

...and my left finger to press the tape down...

Are we keeping you awake Moe?

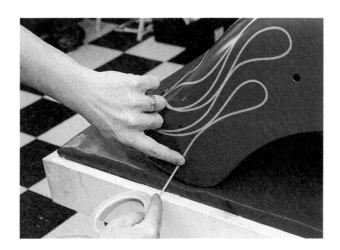

...I get a nice smooth flowing edge.

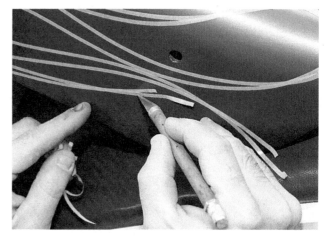

I cut off the overlapping tape on the flame's tips with a new Xacto blade.

68

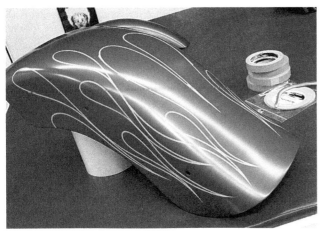

All tips are trimmed so now it's time to mark the flames.

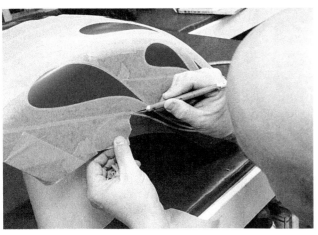

I use the FBS Auto Graphix tape because I can see my 1/8 inch tape through it, and...

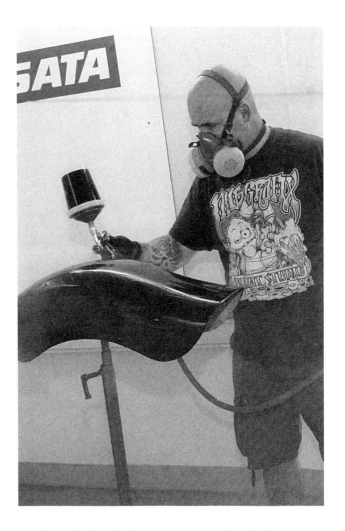

Back to the Booth! Time to mix up the Black basecoat and spray all the areas that aren't taped out.

...it's extremely easy to cut through. Leaving me with a perfectly masked out graphic.

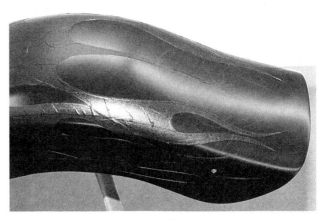

Once I get good coverage, (about 2-3 coats on this one) I let the parts dry for a little bit.

I left that "open area" on the fender because the customer wanted a skull mixed in with the flames.

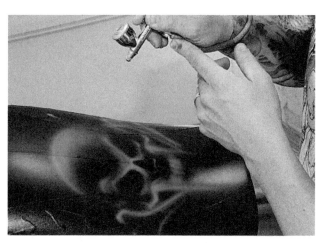

Fogging into the entire skull...color into the entire skull...

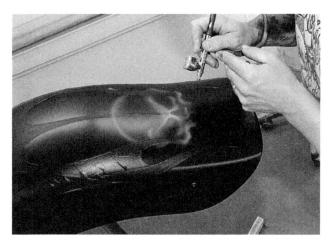

I begin to lay it out with a Medium Tone Blue...

...from top...

I'm just quickly sketching the skull out not worrying too much on adding any detail yet

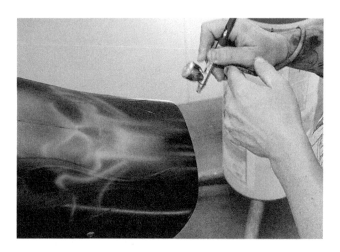

...too bottom...

I add a little loose fiery stuff...

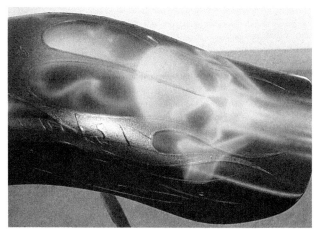

Now that the basic design is fogged in...

...from the top of his head...

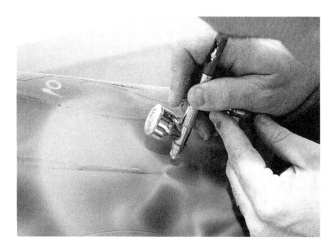

It's time to start adding the details

...to up and behind the taped out flames

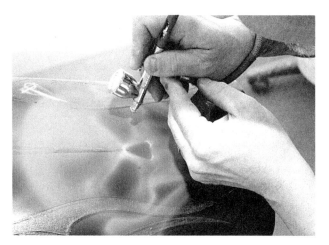

I start with a lighter shade of my original Blue, by mixing in a few drops of white

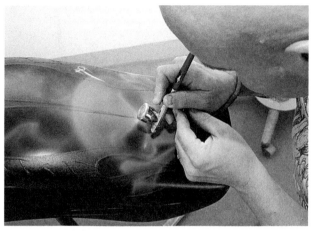

Taking advantage of the whole skull already being blocked in with my medium blue...

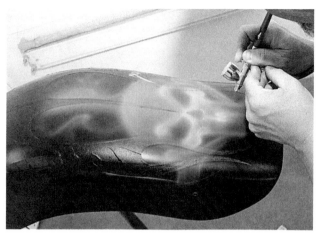

I give some definition to his upper jaw area...

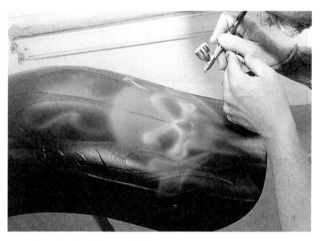

...I slowly build out lighter areas...

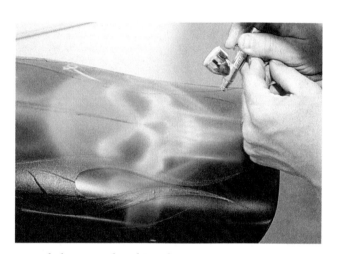

...and those pearly white chompers...

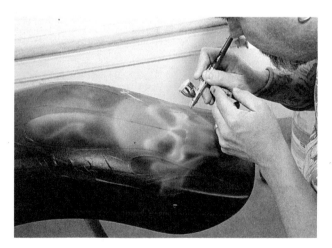

...without completely covering what I've already done.

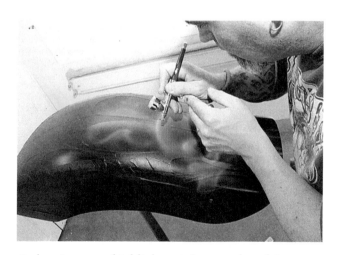

I also give some highlights to the top edge of the skull...

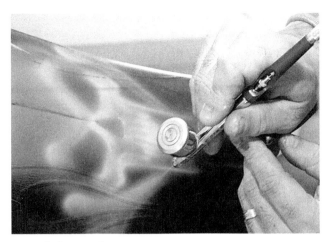

...and the crossbones

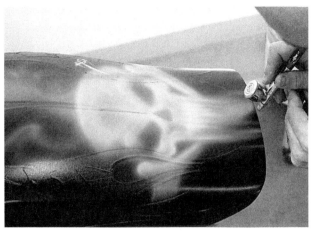

Once my first highlights are blended in, I work on the areas that I feel need to be a bit lighter...

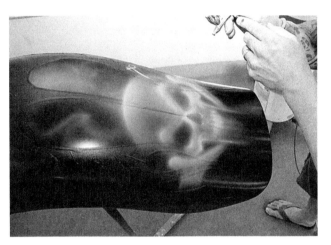

I now pull away from the surface a little bit...

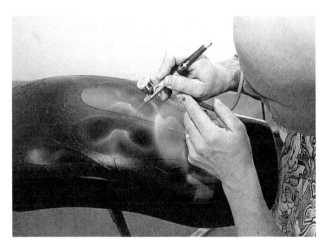

...like the wispy flames...

...to help blend in the highlights

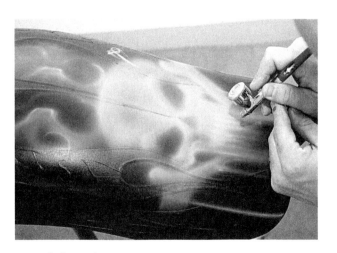

...and those chompers.

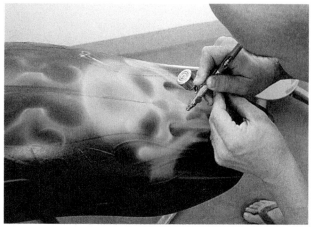

Next, I grab some black with a few drops of blue...

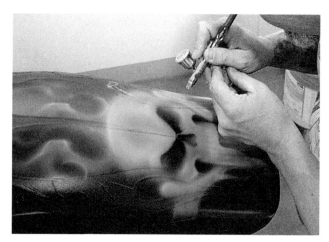

Areas like the eye sockets...

... and begin to reshape my darkest areas

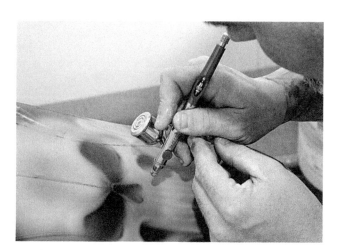

... the nose cavity...

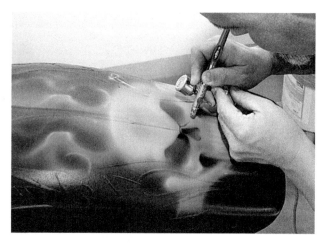

...and give the edges a nice crisp look.

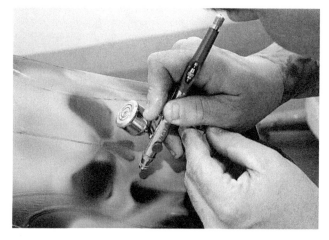

... and the concave area below the cheek bones get the most attention.

Nub - Q&A

Did you always have an artistic knack, were you the kid who could always draw?

Yes, as kid I was always drawing. My mom is an artist, everyone in my family is an artist. I grew up in an artistic environment. I wasn't stifled.

How did you get started painting bikes?

I wanted something different, I was working at a sign shop and my brother bought an airbrush for me, but I didn't use it much. Then I apprenticed for a friend with a body shop. Gradually I did more and more paint work and fewer signs.

How did you hookup with OCC?

I was the body shop in that town, I was four miles down the road. The body shops that painted the first bikes for them just did one-color paint jobs. I partnered up with the guy at the body shop to do paint for OCC, and the paint jobs we did got more and more colorful. The first years, before the TV show, we painted 120 bikes each year. OCC had dealers, it was nuts. I came in pretty green, but as we got busier I realized I could just do artwork. It was insane at the start, we worked 18 hours days. When you are learning a new craft it's good to be challenged, it was a great learning opportunity for me.

How long have you been an airbrush artist?

Like I said, I started airbrushing almost 20 years ago, using it sparingly on the signs, just for highlights and things like that. I slowly got more accustomed to the airbrush and gradually started using it for custom paint. It was 14 or 15 years ago that I started using it almost full time.

Tell us about your typical jobs?

It's funny, when people come in, they all say "I want something different, lets do flames and skulls." So now it's like, how do I do fames and skulls differently? So I talk them into adding some pinstripes and some gold leaf. It's fun to take the run of the mill stuff and make it unique.

Where do you get your ideas?

I get inspired by almost anything, other artists, music, I pull from almost everything I see and hear.

What do you like for materials?

I like AutoGrafix tape, it's my signature tape but it really does work well. I like the way it bends and stays where it's supposed to stay... it's the only product I've ever endorsed like this.

What paint(s) do you typically use?

I jump back and forth between PPG and H of K. I've used the new H of K Shimrin2 for a demo and I like the system. It's great that they finally figured out how to make a paint you can mix yourself.

Do you over-reduce your paint?

I do over reduce big time, I might start with 1 part paint and 2 parts thinner. Then I reduce it more to use in the airbrush so it works the way I want.

How do you pick your colors?

Depends on the job. The older I get the more fond I am of a minimalistic color palette. Grey tones, black and grey, monotone stuff. Color comes natural to me, I learn as I go. I'm always trying to avoid repeating color catastrophes of the past. Just figure out what goes with what. I mix my own colors mostly.

How much do you use the computer?

Mostly for corporate logos. And for portrait work, I use it to map out facial features. It's a great tool if you use it sparingly.

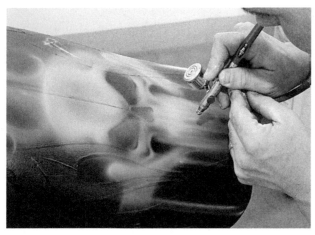

I give a few shadows to the Crossbones to push them behind the skull.

... but this time I use a lighter blue than I did before.

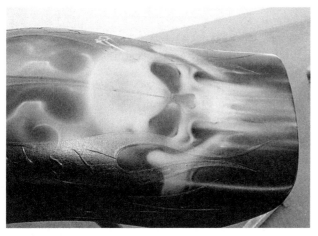

It's good to step back...make sure the dark areas are dark enough.

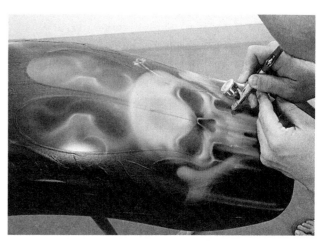

This is why I spend my time working on the Teeth.

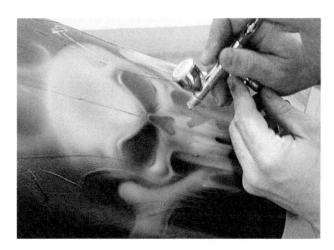

Now it's time to selectively hit my highlights again...

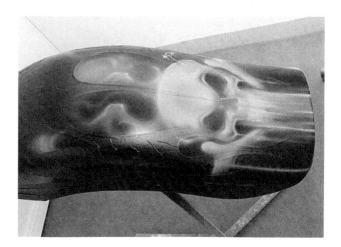

Now step back again to make sure everything is looking balanced...

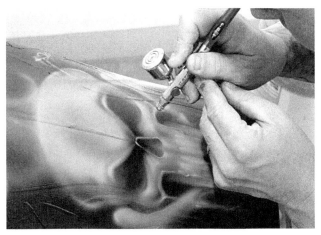

... and then come back in to hit any spots that need more.

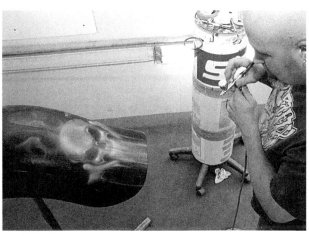

I stipple some white at the bottom to make the skull look like he's shooting out of a star field.

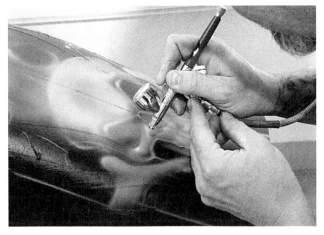

Now I mix a white with only a drop or 2 of blue to do my brightest highlights...

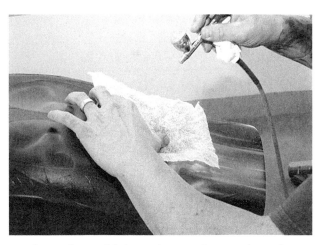

I also grab an old dryer sheet and spray through it by my highlights to give a bit of texture.

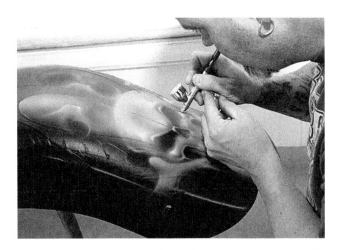

...I use this very sparingly. I don't want to cover all of my darker details I worked on before.

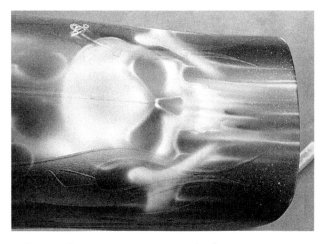

This is where we are at now...a little more to go!

I give tails to some of the stars...

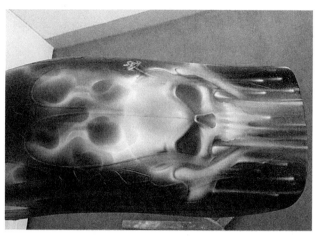

... and then it's on to the next step.

... to help with the feeling of movement.

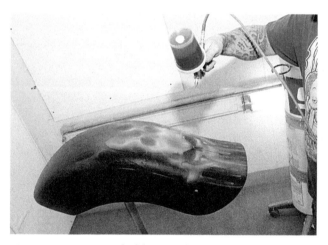

I'm spraying a candy blue wash over the entire piece of artwork.

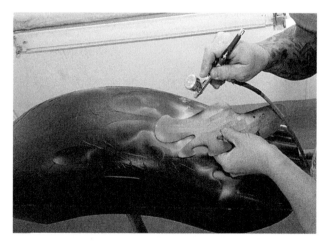

Now a little tightening up of the flame licks...

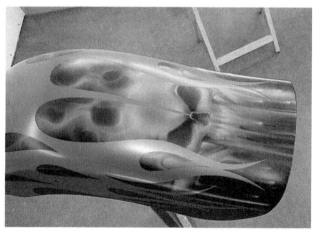

I unmask the flame graphic and we are ready to pinstripe.

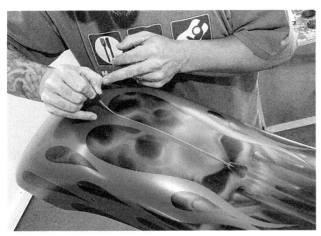

I start my striping in the middle of the panel, working my way out...

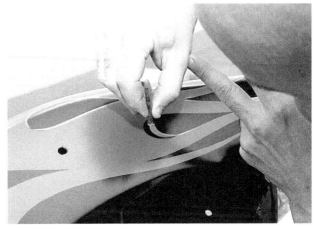

... helps tremendously when you are trying to pull a nice long line...

... and sometimes working a line or two back in.

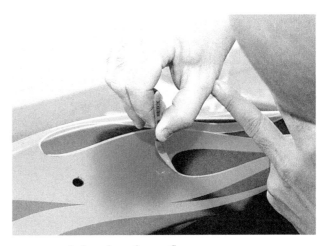

... around the edge of your flame.

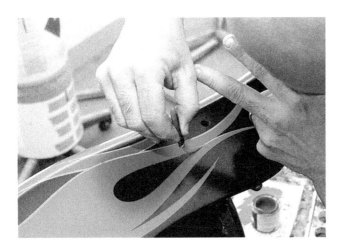

Paint consistency and being in a very comfortable position...

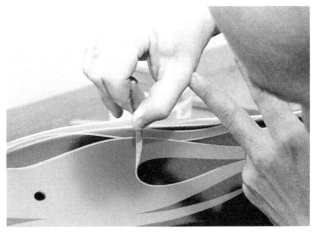

With patience and practice...

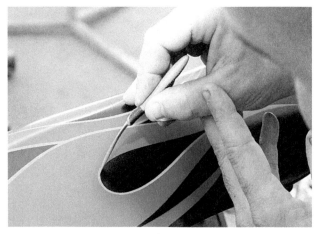

... you will be able to go from the tip of one flame...

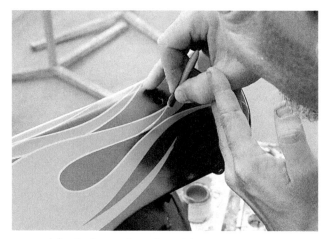

... and back down the other side.

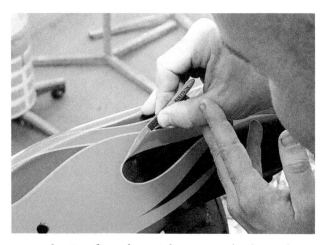

... to the tip of another without even thinking about it.

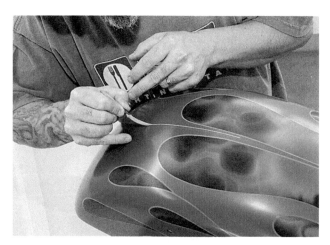

Once all the flames are done being striped...

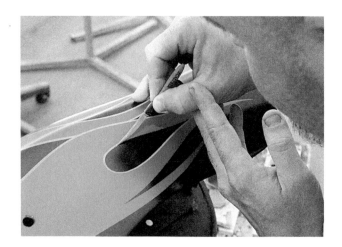

Just steer that brush right through the turn...

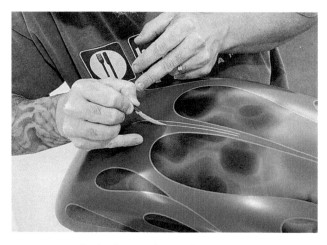

... I start a little design down the center spear.

I'm working again from left to right, right to left.

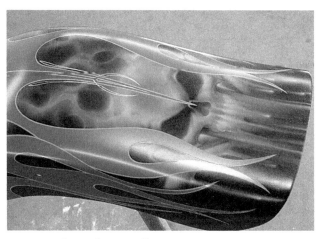

... away from the overall piece.

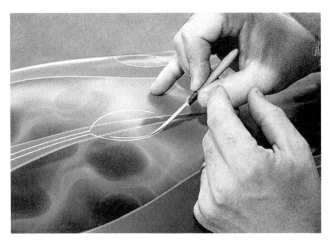

Making sure I keep my design balanced.

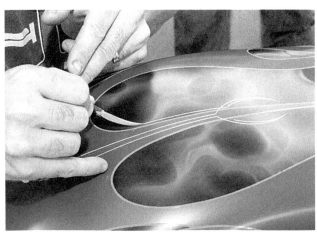

I try to keep this particular design somewhat simple, so it doesn't pull attention...

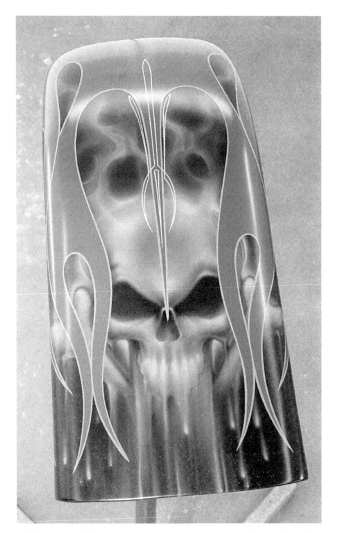

This is it. Time now for clearcoats and then it's off to the happy customer.

Mickey Harris Q&A

The New SATAgraph Airbrush

Before there were airbrush magazines, or books, or artists airbrushing incredible designs on hot rods and Harleys, there were a few intrepid young pioneers in Florida using airbrushes to do crazy designs on T-shirts. Prior to this, airbrushes were used to "airbrush" the pimples off a model's cheek or make the Playboy girls look more like Playboy girls.

Among those pioneers was a young man named Mickey Harris. When he came to work in the T-shirt trade, he had a leg up on the other young artists - he was already a trained artist who understood things like color theory and composition. All he had to do was figure out the airbrush and the rest was easy. Almost forty years later, Mickey is a man with a resume to die for: Featured in hundreds of magazine articles and publisher of Airbrush Magazine; TV credits on Ovehaulin', Car Crazy, Drag Race High and Gearz; member of the Pentagon's Art Program; and painter of many General Motors' special promotional vehicles. In addition to all this, he's also served as a consultant to SATA in the design of their latest airbrush, the SATAgraph 4. All of which makes him the ideal person to talk about what goes into the design and manufacture of a high quality airbrush.

Mickey: Tell us a little about your involvement with SATA on the design of the new airbrush?

I was invited to work with SATA way back, on the SATA 1 and 3. At that time SATA was making air brushes that were designed primarily for intricate detail. The price for these was higher than many professionals or beginners wanted to spend for their collection of brushes. They may have purchased one of them, but had lesser priced air brushes for many day to day projects. We agreed that SATA would

someday like to find a solution that combined good detail ability and fast work speed at a lower price. So we left it at that. Recently though, we got involved again when SATA decided to do something more competitive, and ramp up the airbrush program.

Because I have 36 years of experience they asked for help and we looked at all the good points in the other brands, and then we went through the new SATA gun piece by piece. From

the start, SATA made it clear they did not want to compromise anywhere.

When you actually got to designing the new SATA airbrush, what are some of the changes and improvements that were made, as opposed to other brands and even the earlier SATA airbrushes?

Most modern airbrushes are similar inside, so we went through the new gun piece by piece, and asked ourselves, how can we improve this part? Let's start with the nozzle shield, which has four slots that allow the air to escape when you're working close to the surface. Otherwise you get a vortex and distortion of the line you're spraying when getting close for very fine lines. And it's reversible so you can flip it and screw it back on so that it allows the tip of the needle to stick out so you can pick dried paint off the tip. Most all professionals like the tip exposed.

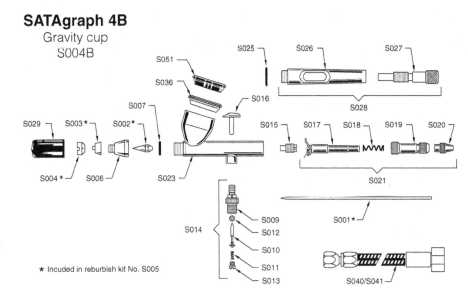

SATAgraph 4B
Gravity cup
S004B

★ Incuded in reburbish kit No. S005

This blow up, and the parts list below, shows each part in the new SATA airbrush. And the photo sequence shows how all the part go together to make one complete, ready to spray, airbrush.

PART ID	SATAgraph 4 Airbrush Spare Parts
S001	airbrush needle
S002	nozzle tip (fluid tip)
S003	nozzle cap (inner air cap)
S004	nozzle cap shield (outer aircap nozzle shield reversible)
S005	needle/nozzle refurbish kit (includes 001, 002, 003, 004)
S006	nozzle base
S007	nozzle base o-ring
S008	nozzle base wrench
S009	air valve chamber
S010	trigger valve stem
S011	trigger valve spring
S012	air valve seal / o-ring
S013	air valve screw
S014	complete air valve assembly (includes 009, 010, 011, 012, 013)
S015	inner seal screw and ptfe o-ring (gravity and side cup models)
S016	airbrush trigger
S017	needle alignment tube and lever assembly
S018	needle tube spring
S019	spring tension adjustment screw
S020	needle locking nut
S021	needle alignment and adjustment assembly (includes 017, 018, 019, 020)
S022	bottom (siphon) feed airbrush body
S023	gravity feed airbrush body
S024	side feed airbrush body
S025	airbrush handle o-ring
S026	trigger stop set handle, red

PART ID	SATAgraph 4 Airbrush Spare Parts
S027	trigger stop set screw
S028	trigger stop set handle and screw (includes 026, 027)
S029	protective nozzle cover
S030	33mm metal jar adaptor for siphon
S031	33 mm 3/4 oz. jar w/ blank storage lid for siphon
S032	33mm metal jar adaptor w/ 3/4 oz. glass jar, siphon
S033	1/4 oz. color cup (siphon cup-metal)
S034	side feed metal color cup
S035	side feed inlet plug, red
S036	metal color cup lid for side and gravity feed color cup
S037	metal side feed jar adaptor for 20 mm jar
S038	1 oz. 20 mm side feed glass jar w/ blank storage lid
S039	metal side feed jar adaptor and 1 oz. glass jar
S040	6 foot braided air hose 1/8 inch X 1/4"
S041	10 foot braided air hose 1/8" X 1/4"
S042	6 foot braided air hose w/ moisture trap
S043	10 foot braided air hose w/ moisture trap
S044	In-line moisture trap
S045	8 foot quick dis-connect braided air hose
S046	quick disconnect plug/fitting,
S047	33mm FastBlast pvc Jar adaptor
S048	33mm FastBlast pvc jar adaptor w/ 3/4 oz. glass jar
S049	pvc lid for 1/4 oz metal siphon color cup
S050	Quick dis-connect air coupler threaded for hose
S051	PVC color cup lid on Gravity feed (B) and Side feed (S).
S004B	SATAgraph 4 B Gravity feed airbrush
S004S	SATAgraph 4 S Side-feed airbrush
S004H	SATAgraph 4 H Bottom-feed siphon airbrush

Each part in the new SATAgraph 4 is both available and affordable.

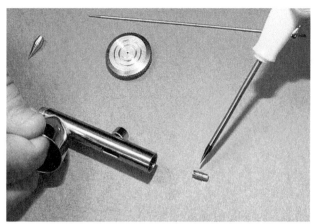

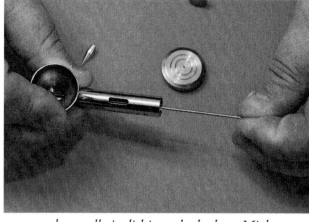

The first part to be installed in the body is the hollow inner seal screw and O-ring (the small O-ring is already installed in the inner seal screw).

... now the needle is slid into the body so Mickey can check the amount of drag on the needle. The seal screw can be tightened or loosened to increase or decrease the drag, and affect the "fit" of the needle.

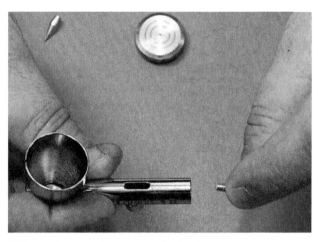

The seal screw drops into the body...

Next to be installed is the nozzle tip (aka: fluid tip)...

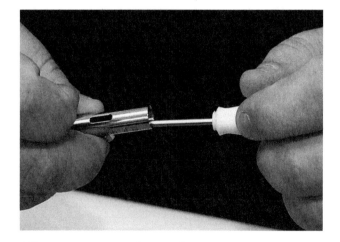

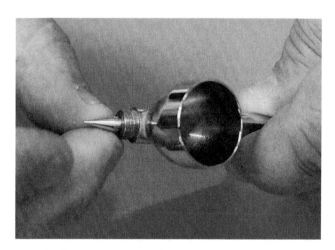

The screw is snugged into place...

... which just slips into place.

We've changed the nozzle base too. This one has six holes, some have just a couple. By having more holes the air is dispersed more evenly.

Even the nozzle-base O-ring was scrutinized. It's made of siliconized-Teflon, so it's soft enough to seal and tough enough to last. It's also OK for water or solvent-based paint and won't cause a reaction with any solvents or paints.

The trigger design is unique too. There's a step in the trigger to make it easy to grip. And the trigger is coated with Teflon where it interfaces with the rocker – part of the needle alignment tube. And the rocker itself is coated in Teflon too, which gives you an easy, smooth trigger pull.

With most airbrushes, if you get the alignment tube twisted, the rocker arm behind the trigger can fall down into the gun, jamming the trigger. So we redesigned it, changing the length and pivot, a change that eliminates the possibility for that to fall down into the gun, I had a lot to do with that part of the re-design.

They redesigned the rear handle too, so it includes an adjustable trigger stop. That's a nice feature for beginning artists, so they can stop the trigger at certain point, and keep the line size consistent.

Mickey, do you want to say something about trouble shooting for the new SATAgraph?

Well, typically, the trouble is all in the front of the gun, with any gun or airbrush. It's always in the head assembly, where the needle makes contact with fluid tip needle.

What I've seen lately is dirty nozzle bases. Dry paint accumulates on the inside of the hole in the base, and people think the gun is wearing out. All you have to do is use a toothpick or nozzle cleaning needle from SATA, and clean the cap. Then it's like a new gun. Don't use abrasive brushes or drill bits as they will damage the hole. Somehow this is the last place people look for trouble.

But overall, I think this new airbrush is very durable. In fact, the changes we made were aimed at making the airbrush more durable, and smoother to operate. If you do need parts, every piece is made in the USA, which makes it easy to find the parts you need on short notice.

The nozzle base O-ring...

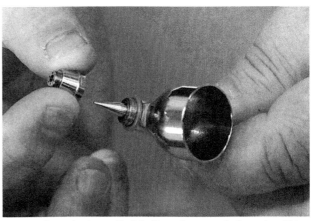

... needs to be installed before the nozzle base itself is screwed onto the body. (Dried paint on the back side of the nozzle base will affect the pattern - a problem the is often misdiagnosed.)

... and tightened with the supplied wrench.

The nozzle cap screws onto the end of the nozzle base...

... as shown, before the slotted...

... and reversible nozzle cap shield is attached.

At this point we have the front of the body and related components assembled.

The air valve assembly is next...

... starting with the air valve chamber, (note O-ring shown installed on trigger valve).

With the O-ring already in place on the trigger air valve stem, the stem is slipped into place.

This very small trigger valve spring is next...

... followed by the air valve screw...

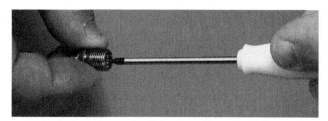

... which is tightened with a small screw driver.

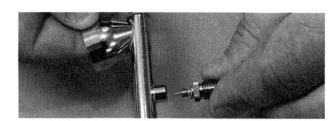

Now the assembled air valve assembly is attached to the body.

The trigger needs to be set into the body...

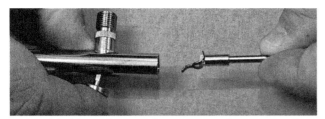

... and held in place as shown as Mickey inserts the needle alignment tube and rocker.

Note how the long art of the rocker protrudes from the top of the body.

The needle tube spring can be slipped into place next.

The needle tension adjustment screw...

... is threaded into the body now.

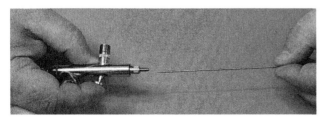

Followed by the needle itself.

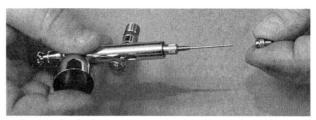

The needle locking nut, accessible from the cutout in the body... .

... threads onto the end of the tension adjustment screw.

The anodized trigger stop set handle threads onto the body. You have to be sure the handle ends up...

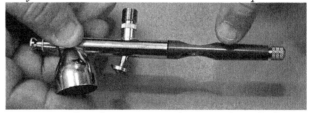

... positioned as shown, so you don't accidentally bump the needle locking nut while using the airbrush.

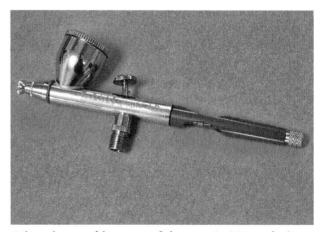

Though assembling one of the new SATAgraph 4 airbrushes might seem a little intimidating at first, it's really just a matter of taking a little time and following directions.

Chapter Six

Tracy Hilgers - TJ Design

A New Spin on Real Fire

Tracy is a man blessed with an abundance of both talent and energy. After watching him in action for a few days, you want to ask just what he puts on those Cheerios in the morning. And it's that little bit of extra energy, that intensity, that makes him strive to do work that is more than just good, more than just OK, more than just nice. Tracy wants to be the best in the region – period.

Though the shop does a variety of work, including automotive restorations and some commercial work for a display company, it's the custom paint and airbrush work done mostly on

The finished panel with clearcoats - think of the sequence that follows as a TJ Design approved short cut to really colorful, real fire.

motorcycles, that keeps Tracy happily working his twelve hour days.

There are two shops at TJ Design, an upper shop where most of the restoration work takes place, and a lower shop, with office and spray booth. Obviously it's the lower shop where you're likely to find Tracy hard at it, starting in the early hours of the morning and still rockin' until well after the sun dips below the horizon.

Those experts who say that men can't muti-task have never seen Tracy at work. The phone rings non-stop and there's all this work to do. So Tracy has the obvious answer, airbrush and talk at the same time. The multi-tasking and long work days mean that Tracy and crew crank out an impressive amount of work from what are really just two, small shops with a total of three bodies.

From traditional flames to real flames to graphics done in shades of gray, Tracy's designs are not easily categorized. Bring in a Panhead and you get a traditional set of flames or graphics. Bring a Buell and you're likely to get something totally different.

Because TJ Design is a full body and paint shop, Tracy can do more than just airbrushing, more than just custom paint. From repairing the dented fender to doing the prep work; from doing the graphics and paint to applying the clearcoats, everything is done in house. Which means Tracy controls the quality from beginning to end, and can ensure it meets his high standards. And for Tracy quality is what it's all about.

Shown here are two short, start-to-finish sequences painting panels that will become display pieces for the TJ Design booth at the next bike show. First is a new twist on how to create real fire. Though most painters follow a long, multi step process using many colors, Tracy has developed his own means of creating very believable real fire, without using ten or more separate colors. And the other display panel is pair of skulls, painted partly with stencils, that morph into a long set of bevelled flames. As you'll see from this chapter, Tracy is one of those artists who make difficult painting projects look simple - like, "it's easy, anybody can do this."

I start laying out the fire with the airbrush working freehand.

Once I have some basic shapes I use a stencil to create a bevelled effect...

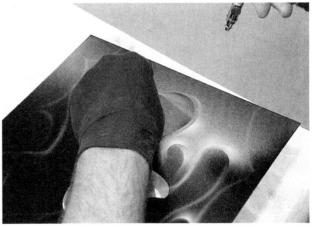

... which helps to give the flames that 3-D appearance.

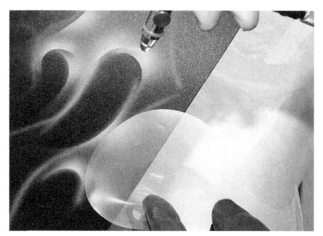

The base is black with ice pearl...

More work with the stencil for that 3-D effect.

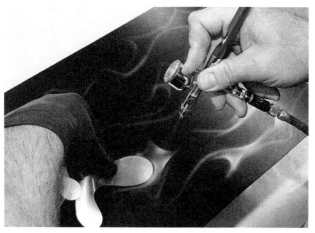

... the initial flames are done with silver fire.

Here I start adding extra freehand filler...

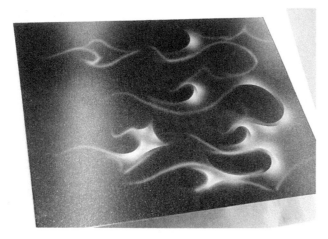

Progress shot, the panel looks good but there's more to do.

... the freehand work gives the fire a softer feel...

... so the fire doesn't look so much like a sticker or decal.

Again, the initial layout is done freehand...

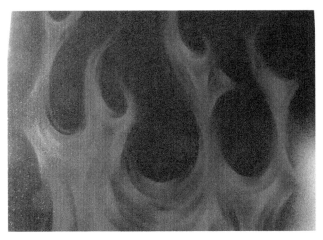

After the first layer is done, I add a coat of Kandy Apple Red.

... then I bring in the stencil.

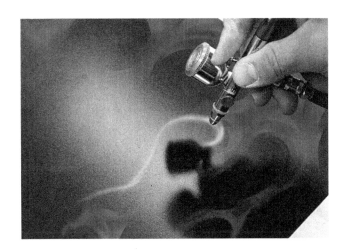

Now the process repeats...

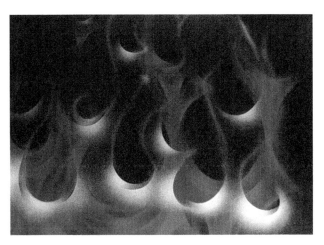

Be sure you don't add your second layer directly over the first.

Slowly I work across the panel with my stencils, adding details and enhancing the bevelled effect.

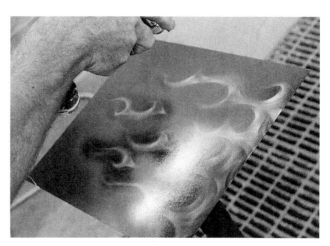

... or you can add some kandy gold over it...

ext I soften the edges by working across the panel free-hand.

Here's the second layer, the results look cool and you could stop here...

... which gives it that look of real fire.

Tracy Hilgers, Q&A

Tell us about the other painting you do, and the typical jobs that come through the shop?

Of the work that comes in, a strong seventy percent is motorcycle painting and of that almost 90 percent is something custom with graphics that I do with an airbrush. The other thirty percent of our work is restoration work.

How long have you been an airbrush artist?

Airbrushing was a natural progression for me, when I started I was doing custom painting of sport bikes, but I quickly realized there's no money in that. So I started doing more restorations. Then I met Neil from American Thunder and started doing a lot of work for them, and most of that was custom paint jobs with flames and graphics. That is when I started doing more airbrushing.

Where do you get your ideas, who or what inspires you?

Some from previous jobs, some from Google, some from other people's work. Ideas just come to me sometimes, or I take an idea and tweak it, build on an earlier idea, either mine or someone else's.

What paint(s) do you typically use for the airbrushing?

I use H of K and PPG automotive paints.

Do you over-reduce the paint when you use it in an airbrush?

Yes, though it depends on what I'm doing. If it's a typical 1 to 2, ratio, I do 1 to 5 or 1 to 4. But if you go too far, you get blow-outs.

How much do you use the computer, can you give us an example?

I probably use the computer for 30 percent of my business. Some of that is plotter work, and masks. I also do lot of hand work. Most of my masks are drawn and cut by hand. The computer is really handy for stencils and lettering.

If there was no customer involved, what kind of paint jobs would you do?

My favorites are highly complex paint jobs. It's a love-hate thing really. I love it when I'm doing one. Highly detailed, multi layered, very three dimensional looking. My favorite is to create a paint job that will just stop people in their tracks and have them wonder, "How did he do that." My truck is the one thing that I've done where I get that question all the time. At the World of Wheels show there were over a hundred people who stopped, stared and asked, "How'd you do it? That was one of the awards I won - for Prestigious Paint on that truck.

Flames & Skulls

The four small images show how I use a combination of skull stencils, and freehand work, to get started on the one-color project.

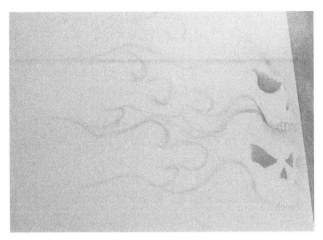

This is my basic layout.

Once I have the basics done, I go in for some of the finer details.

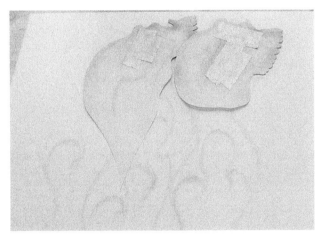

I made these stencils, and use them now to establish my outline...

On this job I used a straight white panel with reduced black paint.

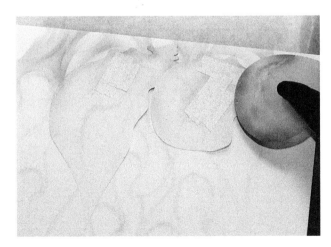

With a little additional help from a second, hand-cut stencil.

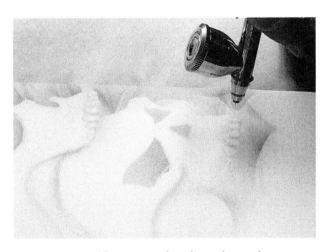

Here I start adding more details to the teeth.

I'm gonna give him an angry look with some detail between the eyes.

I keep coming back to add more and more detail to the teeth.

Here I'm trying to create a cheek bone...

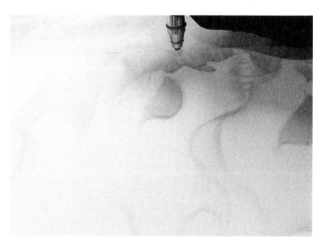

I'm trying to make the skull pop a little more by making the leading edge darker.

... and do the same thing on the other side of his face.

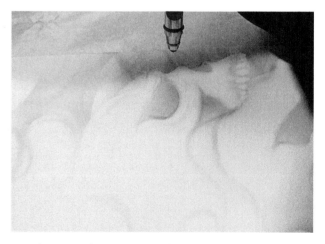

Working on the eyes, with detail on the edges...

... before darkening the eye sockets themselves.

This is the image, essentially finished.

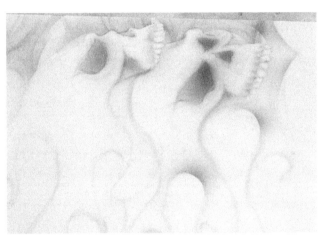

Here you can see the effect of the details I've added to the teeth and the eyes.

With a stencil I'm adding detail to his face, next I will enhance the flames.

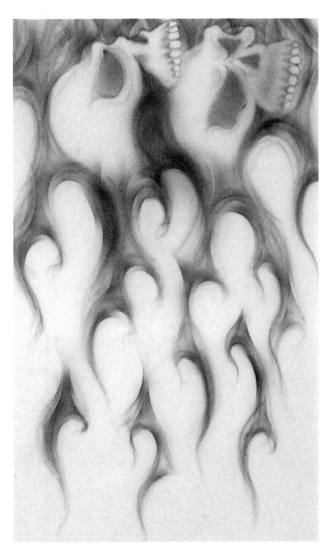

And this is the image after I darkened the grays and blacks, and covered it with a coat of flat clear.

Chapter Seven

Andy Anderson

Tragedy Sparks Creativity

Andy Anderson makes his living as a screen printer, operating Anderson Studios in Nashville, Tennessee. But anytime things are slow, or Andy can steal a few free minutes, he heads for his hideout. Andy's hideout isn't a bar and it isn't an entertainment room. In fact, Andy's hideout looks a lot like a paint shop.

Located deep in the lower level of the Anderson Studio shop is a small body and paint shop. This is where he hides. Building custom

I was presented with a project: a memorial to family members lost tragically. The art was very personal so I wanted it to be right. Like I said it's very personal - a woman crying over the loss of two loved ones.

motorcycles, performing the necessary body and prep work, and doing the paint jobs.

Andy started painting and customizing bikes when those bikes had pedals for power and the paint came out of what we call a rattle can. From rattle-can paint jobs on Schwinns he rapidly graduated to metal-flake and old-skool lace chopper paint jobs when those were still new.

Though he's been known to build complete motorcycles, Andy's real passion is paint. Equally comfortable with either a full size spray gun, or an airbrush, Andy paints for a small group of customers and shops. Other than occasional help from his life long friend Clyde, Andy is pretty much a one-man band working away in the shop with only the stereo for company.

With a lifetime's worth of experience painting motorcycles and designing T shirts, Andy is equally happy working from the customer's design, or doing one of his own. In the case of the airbrush design seen here, Andy started with the customer's rendering, which he modified to better fit the fender. Next came the scan then the use of a plotter to cut out the elaborate masks. Additional, very small masks were cut out by hand as needed during the paint job.

If there are two things Andy's paint jobs are known for, it's incredible color and tight, tight details. Guns and Roses is no different. Consider the fact that the fender itself is only about seven inches wide. Then take a good look at the face, the petals, the guns themselves. You can see every tear, every highlight on every petal, and every screw on each of the pistols.

Like a lot of "airbrush" artists, Andy often uses a small brush to fill in details too small to be done with the airbrush.

When the multiple masks and dozens of layers are complete, Andy is able to do the clearcoat and the polishing in his own shop - one of the advantages of having a complete shop and paint booth is maintaining complete control of the project, and never having to wait on another shop to finish their part of the job.

To get an accurate reference to work from I photographed a real 38.

Fender width was measured and a rough comp was rendered after my pencil sketch in the computer.

The rendering was printed out using our color printer. This allowed me to cut and remove parts as needed. The customer wanted the face in the middle so I tore it out and moved it into the center of the design.

This is the final design I did for the customer's approval. From here it was plotted and cut to a vinyl mask.

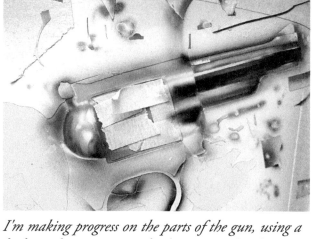

I'm making progress on the parts of the gun, using a little masking tape to go back over an edge that needed more work. Colors are HOK Shimrins mixed as needed.

This photo shows the vinyl mask. Rubbing sign-painter's pounce chalk over the cut lines makes them easier to see.

With one gun nearly done I begin duplicating the same steps on the other. There are some minor differences that I've had to make because of the difference in the right and left side of a gun.

This photo shows the different components of the mask. I have pulled an area on the gun to start my airbrushing. The base is showing through the pulled area.

Right side just about finished. More detail will be added in the final steps of the complete painting.

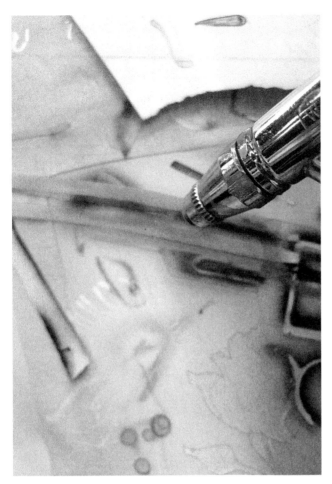

Regular masking tape...

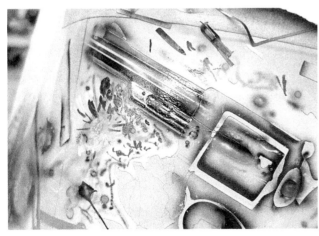

... comes in handy for straight line work.

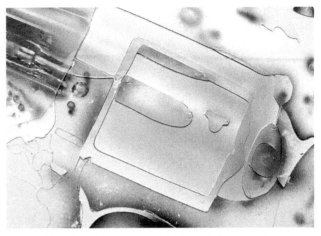

Here the chamber is unmasked and I started airbrushing the grays. I work light to dark then go back and add hi-lights..

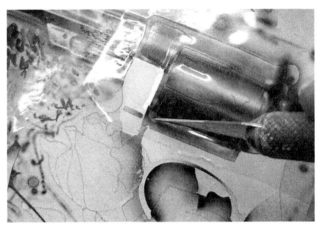

In the case there's a correction due to the original not being cut right I simply mask the area with Frisket (shown as a shiny clear film) and cut the areas I need to airbrush.

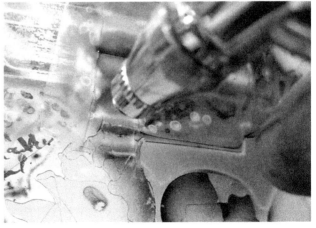

This is a close up of some of the tight areas I had to airbrush. This was smaller than 1/4 inch.

Both guns are pretty much complete. Notice all the cut out vinyl pieces around the art. It's like a puzzle. Remove some -paint the area, put the pieces back and move on to another area.

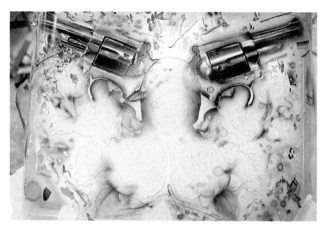

Here you can see some of the leaves are shaded (the ones on the right) - on the left ones I'm in the process of adding the shadows....

I begin to color the parts of the roses, starting with the stems and leaves.

... the main mask is still in place over the face and roses.

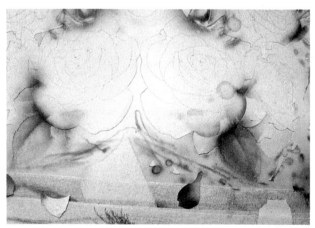

I mixed several shades of green and began with a light green. I work light to dark and mix by eye. I've painted this way for over 40 years so it's not a problem for me to duplicate a color formula by eye.

I use 2 or 3 shades of mixed pink for the roses. Highlight areas are masked during the process and uncovered after all the color is in place. I then add a tint as needed to the petals.

The left rose is just about finished. The one on the right has some of the areas masked for airbrushing the shadows around the petals.

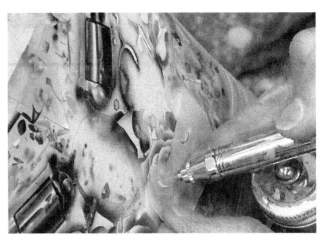

I sometimes add detail with hand cut stencils.

This photo shows the hi-lights left on the top edge of the petals for detailing later.

Still more roses to airbrush but I'm making progress.

Some final close up details added to the high lights on the petals. Notice the art reference taped above the work. This was my final comp that I referred to during my painting process.

Making good progress on the roses.

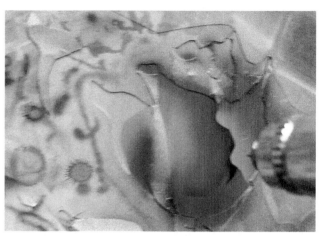

Edge of a petal mask is pulled to reveal the depth that the shadow makes on the rose.

Close up of shading on a rose bud. It's just attention to form and details here. I work light to dark pink.

Almost finished with the roses.

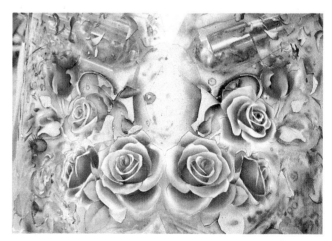

This photo shows the completed roses. Now I'm ready to reverse mask the roses, save them and move on to the face.

Now I'm starting on the face. I begin with my lightest flesh color and then add details to the lips, eyes and nose.

This photo shows a piece of my hand-cut mask used on the details of the roses.

The face is started with a light skin tone I mixed for the base. I used 3 different skin colors and add some pink to add warmth and lip color.

The finished roses.

The area I'm working on is the size of a dime - the detail is very tight. I used a magnifier to see better. The vinyl plotter can't cut some of these small areas so I had to do a lot of tiny hand-cut stencils.

More work strengthening the flesh tones and adding detail.

Now I feel I'm close.

I'm not happy with the eyes, nose and lips. I added some hand brush work and it's too harsh and looks out of place. So I have to go back over these areas with some more airbrush detail work.

So I've removed the mask around the hair to see how it's looking. I'll put the mask I saved of the face back on and begin working on the hair.

Working on my face details and corrections.

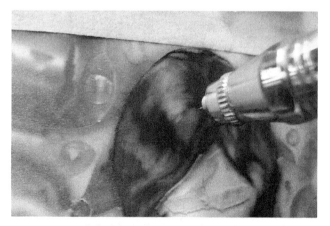

Again I work light to dark on the hair color and detail. I'm careful to leave highlights in the hair when airbrushing the color.

I added a little detail to the hi-lights of the hair with a brush. Being careful to not overdo the detail.

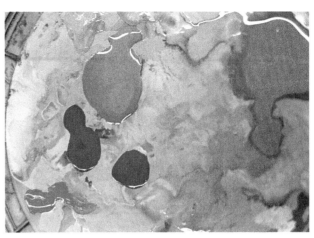

Here's my color palette for my skin tones and touch ups.

Stepping back to look at the hair I'm ready to pull my outside mask and add several coats of clear.

This next step I've sanded my clear and started work on all the touchups and details.

The mask has been pulled and I've cleared the art with 3 coats of HOK urethane clear.

The customer requested 2 tears running down the girl's face. I did 3 versions using a tiny fine hair brush and a magnifier ...

107

... here's a close up of the tear. Still too heavy for my liking so I did one more version.

In this photo I have toned down the tears - I made them a lot more subtle by toning the highlights back with a little skin color so the tears appear softer and more natural looking.

Overall photo of the work. Still more detail to add.

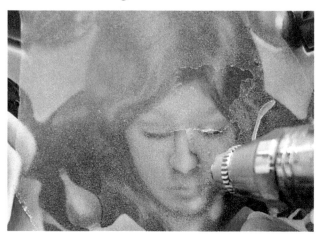

At this point the nose needs some work to improve the shape.

I paint a lot of the very small details by hand, using a very fine brush and these paints, which have been mixed by eye from H of K Shimrin2 materials.

Getting closer here. Tears are finished, but the lips and nose will require more attention before I'm finished.

Airbrushing a very light highlight to the upper lip using a hand mask.

At this point the tears are more natural and very subtle...

By coating the piece with water it's easier to see areas that need more work.

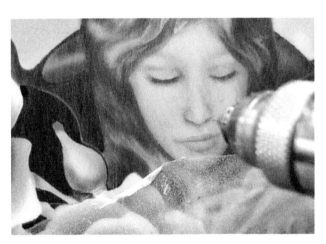

... the lips are looking good and this last detail added to the shadow of the nose will complete the job.

The finished piece with the final pinstripes and clear.

Chapter Eight

John Hartnett

An Old Skool Goldleaf and Pinstripe Project

Mark Shadley, the owner and builder of the sheet metal seen here, has known John Hartnett for a long time, and describes him simply as, "an all around crafty kind of guy. When it comes to pinstripes or graphics or flames, John can do it all." And when Mark says All, he means everything. John started out doing pinstripes on funny cars and other race cars, and today he continues to paint and stripe hot rods of all types. The painting itself is sometimes done in

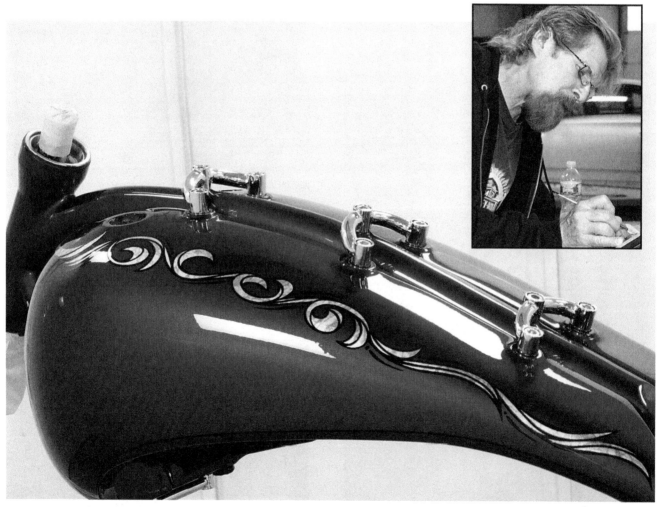

A set of custom tanks on a Shadley Brothers creation, complete with a period-correct goldleaf and pinstripe design.

John's own small shop, though much of his work, like the custom Sportster tanks seen here, are done at someone else's shop. Especially with bigger vehicles, like commercial trucks, John prefers to work in a shop bigger than his own.

John's craftyness extends to flame jobs of every flavor, and complete paint jobs on both cars and motorcycles. And though John does a variety of work on every type of vehicle imaginable, it's motorcycles that are the one constant. Whether the two wheeler needs pinstripes, flames, graphics, or goldleaf, John is the man.

Motorcycles not only take up much of John's working hours, they also occupy much of his free time. Weekends often find John and his wife off on some trip to nearby Connecticut on their individual Harleys.

There was a time when John did the gypsy painting thing, renting booths at events like Daytona Beach Bike Week. But it's a lot of travel and a lot of work; and John already has a list of regular clients as long as your arm, so what's the point?

Today, John is much more likely to spend his week days driving from shop to shop in towns like Whitman and Hanson, Massachusettes. Painting and striping custom bikes on one day and a new tow truck the next. And weekends on his two-wheeler thinking about anything but work.

A piece of tape will locate the sketch to come.

The sketch itself starts with the paper positioned on the tank...

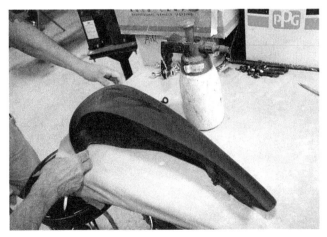

John starts with one of the tanks, already wiped down with wax and grease remover.

... and is finished up on the bench...

111

... where it's easier to draw out all the details.

... with a pencil. Because of the Saral paper underneath, the design...

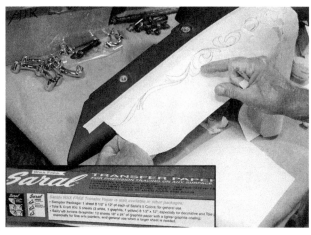

John repositions the finished sketch and slips a piece of Saral paper under the sketch.

... is transferred to the tank.

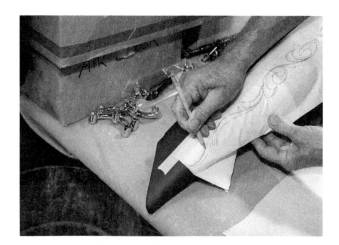

Now he traces over the design again...

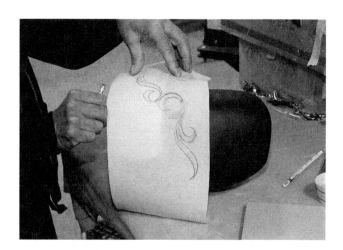

The same technique...

... is used to continue the design to the front of the tank.

... "so you can see where you're putting the size, otherwise it's transparent."

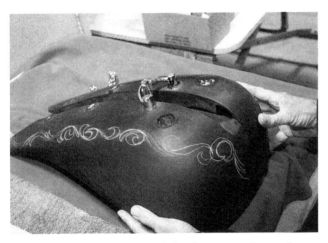

John checks the position of the design on the tanks before getting ready to apply the gold leaf.

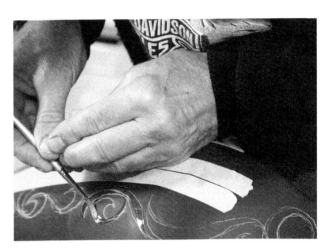

"The size sits for 30 minutes or so, until it's just a little tacky...

The "size" or adhesive, is mixed with One-Shot gold paint...

"I drag a knuckle to get an idea how wet or dry it is, I like it more tacky than dry - unless I'm doing engine turning on the leaf."

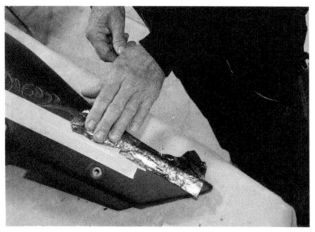

This is variegated leaf which John is putting down.

… to gently pull away the excess goldleaf.

"You don't have to be so careful how you push this down, this variegated leaf is pretty forgiving."

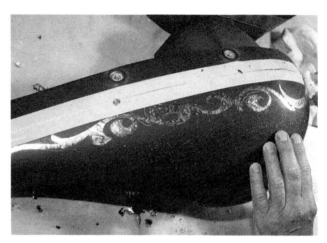

Here's the goldleaf on the tank.

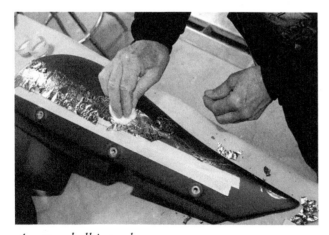

A cotton ball is used...

One cleaned up tank and fender almost ready for pinstripes. The right side tank holds gas, the left side is for oil, which explains the bulge in this right side tank - which increases the fuel capacity.

A coat of intercoat clear was applied before the pin-striping begins.

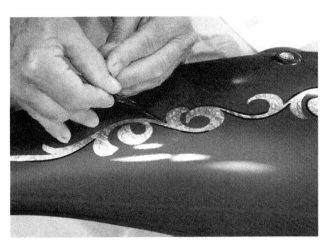

... along both sides...

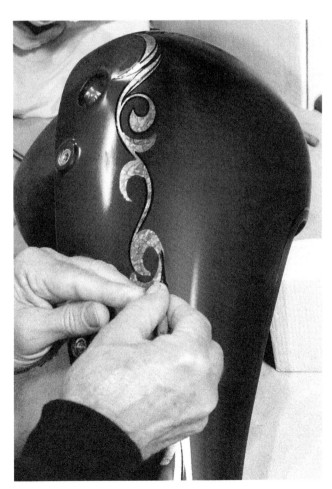

John starts by following the outside edge of the goldleaf...

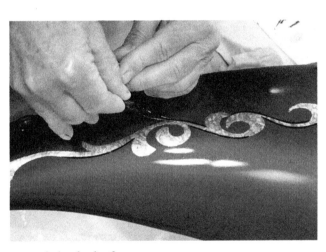

... to help the leaf...

... really stand out.

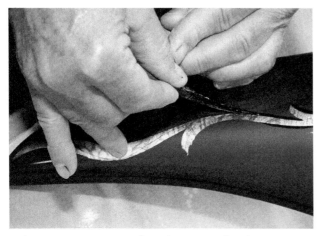

The stripes are painted with House of Kolor paint.

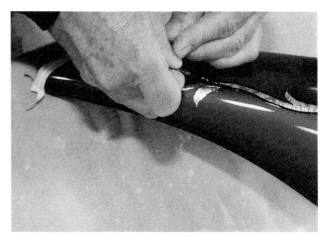

Most of the work is done with a size 00 Mack brush.

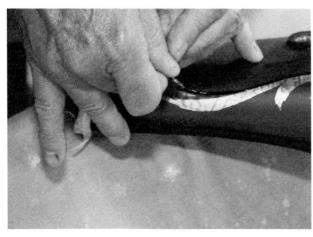

Notice how John uses one hand to support and steady the other.

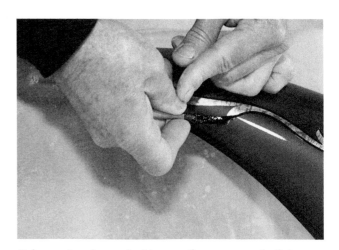

John patiently works his way from one end of the tank to the other...

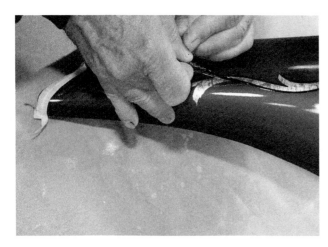

The H of K paint is a urethane, which can be used with or without hardener.

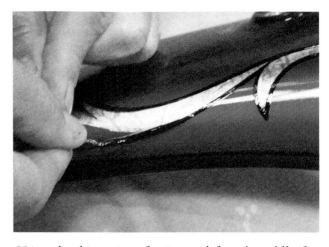

Using the thin stripe of paint to define the goldleaf and clean up the edge.

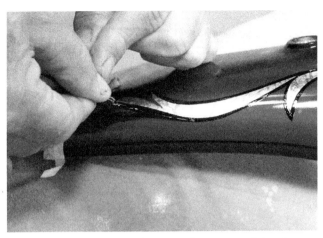

The brush holds enough paint that curves like this...

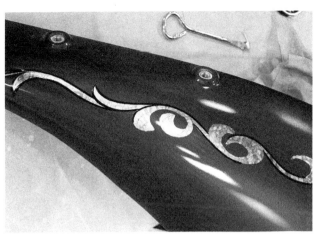

Note how consistent the stripes are...

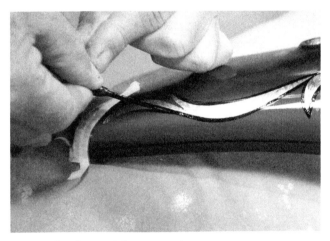

... can be done without stopping.

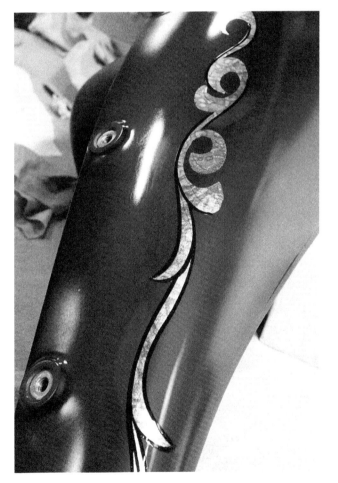

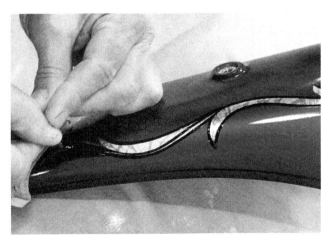

A second line adds a little bit of complexity to the design - the stripes do more than just follow the edge of the leaf.

... the same width all the way through.

117

For curly cues like this...

Getting the paint thinned correctly is one of the keys to good pinstripes, "but with the black, sometimes by the time you get it thinned enough to run a nice line...

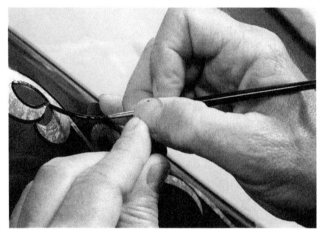

... John likes to use a "liner" in stead of a more typical pinstripe brush...

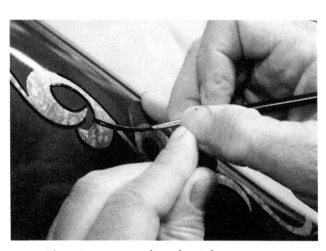

... as it's easier to control in the tight corners.

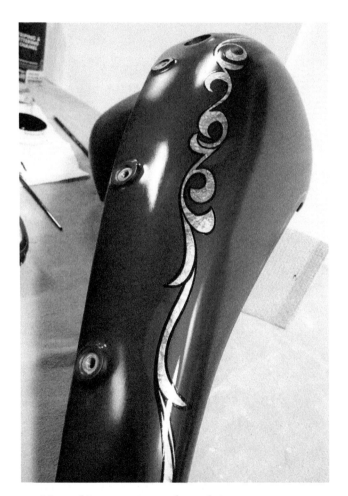

... it's so thin you can see through it...

... so you have to go over the lines twice."

... on the leaf, and below the leaf...

Just a few more accents...

... finish up the job of applying an old skool goldleaf and pinstripe design.

The handmade tanks are part of an Shadley Brothers Ironhead Sportster project, so the old skool flavor of the goldleaf is not only tasteful but very appropriate.

Chapter Nine

Tex McDorman - Tex EFX

The Pinstripe America Tour

Like some of the other illustrious painters seen in this book, Tex found his calling at an early age, thirteen, when he began trying to duplicate the work he saw in various chopper and hot rod magazines. In spite of an interrup-

tion in that career while he served in Uncle Sam's Navy, Tex likes to say, "it seems like I've always been a painter."

Today the heart of the Tex EFX operation is located in Sanger, Texas, just a bit north of

Semi-subtle yet cool without being in your face. Pinstriping flames is one of Tex's specialities, this one was done to have a bit of a throw back look in the design and color choice. Tex even added the accent stripe to the wheels.

Dallas. With help from his son Critter, and long-suffering wife, Melissa, Tex paints, airbrushes and pinstripes everything from motorcycles to Motorhomes and even airplanes. If you can't find him in his Texas shop, it's because he often takes his show, The Pinstripe America Tour, on the road, working a variety of motorcycle and hot rod events all over the country.

In Sturgis, Tex makes his home away from home at the Kick Start Travel Plaza on Hwy 34, on the way to the Buffalo Chip. What's surprising is the fact that he gets any striping at all done while he's there. Not because he doesn't work hard, and not because he parties too much. Rather, because there isn't anyone who drives through that parking lot who doesn't know Tex. Which means there's an endless stream of friends, acquaintances and industry celebrities, all wanting to exchange a greeting with Tex. Which says a great deal about Tex's personality and explains the high number of repeat customers, many of whom have been coming to Tex for their paint and striping for ten and fifteen years.

Among the legions of Tex fans are a few corporate sponsors, including House of Kolor paint, and SATA spray guns. Also, a Texas Vodka company, which is interesting considering the fact that Tex doesn't imbibe.

What Tex does do is paint and paint and paint some more. Pinstripes, flames, and graphics. There simply isn't much that Tex hasn't done and won't do again.

Before starting the entire bike is cleaned with H of K KC10 wax and grease remover.

Sometimes striping the right side of the bike means, doing it from the left side. Notice my paint is thinned and in a non-waxed Dixie cup, I pallet it in the cup.

121

Try not to plan this out to a "T". Instead, let it roll with the contours of each panel and yet, be fluid from front to back.

Occasionally the positions you are in are odd and will cause you to have to finish a particular part of design after you reposition yourself.

I advise beginners to keep the same pressure and stroke rate (speed) throughout the design.

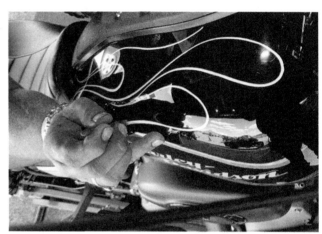

Keep an eye on your drag finger so you don't loose the flow by bumping into those emblems.

I lift up on the brush slightly and slow down at the end of a line, to get the sharp point.

Take pictures in your head or with your phone so you'll have a quick reference for the other side.

Don't get too crazy, sometimes less is more.

If it's easier, take the breather off!

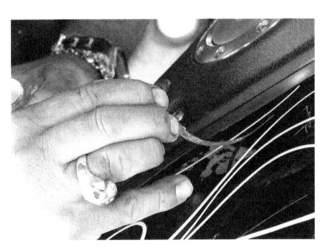

I'm working with wet on wet paint.

I started at the end of the flame working away from my body, I twisted the brush to make the turn and came back towards myself.

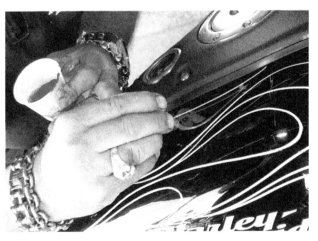

This is extremely tricky since the white paint is still wet. Humm... Where to put my finger (don't go there!)

Notice my right hand is not touching the bike and is supported by my left hand.

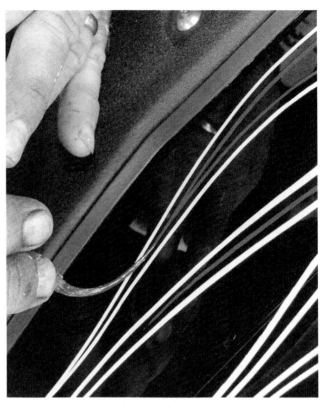

Dont get in a hurry when adding this accent line inside, be consistant in the spacing to the white.

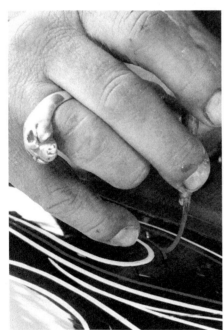

This is a tight turn going away from me and slightly out of my view.

Making this turn you are going to gradually bring your line into the other line you've already done.

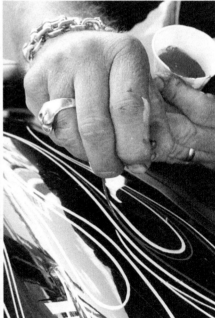

This is a talent to make it flow and not be choppy or noticeable.

It's hard to explain this look to a customer so, make sure you have photo albums to show designs similar to what you want to do on his or hers.

Picture these strokes prior to attempting them, it's going to be hard to wipe it off when the white is wet.

I'm not going to lie, if this was easy.... you wouldn't have bought this book.

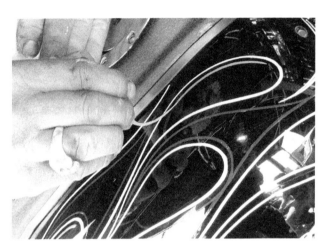

The last little accent, a medium to dark grey accent line - almost like a shadow of the white.

You aren't using a pattern so, stop and start the inside accents where it looks correct.

The front of the bike is on a stand so the tire spins freely. Lock your guide finger in a wheel groove and slowly move the wheel clockwise.

125

Tex EFX, Q&A

A little background on how you became a pinstriper ?

I was lucky to have a famous grandmother who was a canvas artist, and a mother who was a cake artist, so it seemed that art was always in my life. As a kid I was grounded A LOT so it gave me plenty of time to practice the designs I saw in hot rod books and chopper magazines. I started pinstriping at age 13. I striped through high school in Brownwood, Texas and when I graduated, doing it for a living was the farthest thing from my mind. I joined the Navy and got married right out of high school in '82, but I always kept striping and practicing. I got out of the Navy in '92 and decided to go into it fulltime. We had been stationed in the Virginia Beach area for ten years so we opened up our sign and custom shop in Chesapeake and stayed there for another ten years. In 2002 we moved back to Texas and opened McDorman Signs & Advertising, as well as our custom paint division, Tex Efx. It's a family affair with my wife Melissa and our son Critter. It seems like I have always been a pinstriper, it's what I love to do!

What do you like for brushes?

Like most older stripers I started with Mack brushes because you could get them anywhere. Over the years a lot of new companies have come out with new styles and blends of different hairs. Kafka has some great brushes for doing tight turns and curley Qs. Xcaliber has been on the scene with some unique stuff as well. I have really gotten used to, and have been lucky enough to be sponsored by, Lazer Lines. They make a whole host of great brushes with interchangeable handles. They were purchased by Mack a few years ago, so you can get them through Mack.

What paint do you prefer?

I have been with House of Kolor since 1985. In fact, we've been field testing some new formulas and colors for them over the past couple of years.

Tex EFX, Q&A

What about clearing the stripes?

If you use the House of Kolor hardener and reducer, you don't have to clear the stripes. If you are working on basecoat and plan to clear it, the paint works even better. It dries quick and can be cleared with no issues, you only need to use the color and reducer, NO HARDNER, when clearing! Some pinstripers also use One-Shot. It is not, however, friendly to being cleared over!

Do you draw out your designs ahead of time, do you plan the stripe job, or do you just run with it. How do ya proceed?

With some of the more detailed pieces we do in the shop, I will sketch out a few of the lines and then just free-ball the rest. I may have a plan in my mind, but it is subject to change at any second. As I'm going along I often see a picture or design developing by accident, which makes me change my focus or what I want the finished job to look like. When I'm on the road there's no time to draw anything other than a center-line. Time is of the essence, so you tend to get a picture in your mind of what you want this piece to look like. You start with the most contrasting color first, working your way around the project. This is like your rough sketch, each color you add after that compliments the first color as well as body-lines or certain places that need accents.

Are there guidelines or rules in terms of how many times a line should cross another, or how crowded a design should be?

I have definitely seen lines crossing each other too many times and main body lines too crowded by other contrasting colors. This takes time to master, you can have a very busy design with a lot of detail, you can have a lot of lines in close proximity, as long as they flow in the same direction or cross one another with a purpose. When they cross or when they run close together they have to be heading to a certain visual point and be equal on both sides. When you look at it you should be able to tell the visual point and the purpose.

Is Pinstriping all you do at Tex Efx?

Oh no! If anything, I try to be diversified. I pinstripe, do full custom paint on cars, bikes, airplanes, tour busses and big rigs. I airbrush and do hand lettering. We have a sign company that my wife Melissa runs. She is a big part of the reason I got to where I am. Our son Critter also works with us, he is my right hand guy! I couldn't put out half the work around here without him. He takes care of prepping, tear downs and rebuilds and all the other shop stuff while I'm doing artwork

Any words of advice for aspiring pinstripers?

Always treat your business like a profession, be professional! If you give them a little more artwork than they were expecting you will likely get a tip. If you don't get the tip, don't sweat it, they will tell a lot of people how good you are and those people are all potential customers. Whether you are on the road or in your shop, keep your area squared away. Clean and organized is how most customers perceive a professional. Call or email me with any questions, I will help however I can. tex@texefx.com/ texefx@yahoo.com/ 940-367-1433.

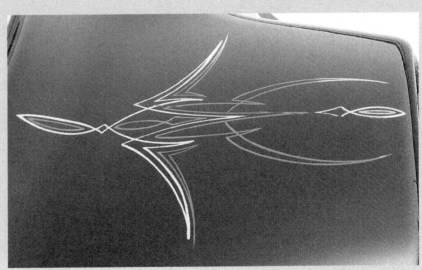

Bike Number Two

"Black Betty" A Colorful Sporty

Tisha Kozloff

This was a really fun job to do at Sturgis this year. All Tisha Kozloff said she wanted was some purple to accent her LED lights, the rest was up to me, "do it like it was your wife's bike" and have fun! There was no time crunch and no real budget, just a price range to keep it under if possible. You will see over the next pages that we put striping in a few out of the ordinary places.

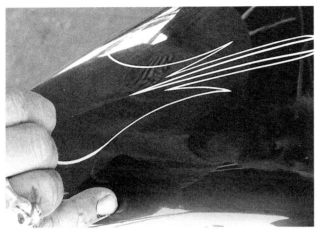

I start with a center line on the tank done with a stabilo pencil. I usually start on the tank with a symmetrical center piece.

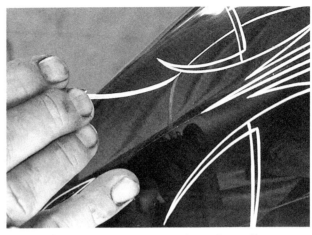

There is absolutely no plan on how this will turn out, that way the customer is surprised with the finished design and so am I.

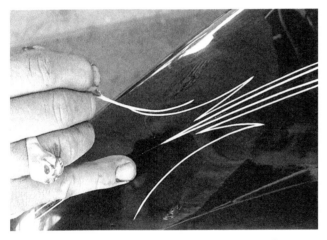

I like to start here on the center, this design often sets the tone for how the rest of the bike will look.

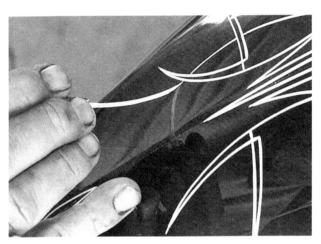

Because I am right handed, I do the first part of the left side of the center line then...

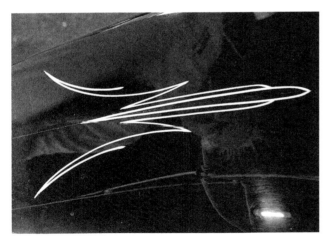

The start is fairly simple in design, it's just getting a starting balance.

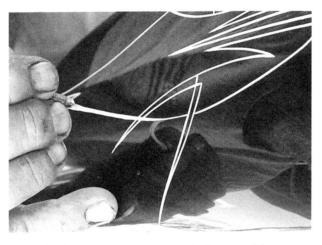

... I duplicate it on the right side because I have a clear view of what I just did.

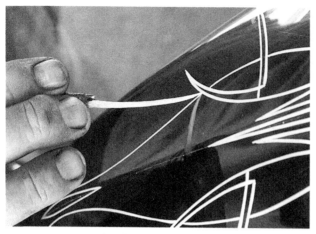

As you can see, the design gets slightly more complex each time you add a stroke.

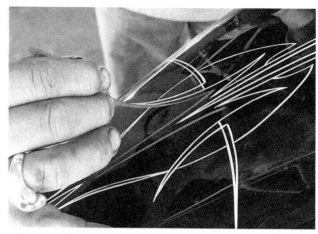

This is where thinking ahead will benefit you. Hopefully you left certain shapes inside your design open for the next colors.

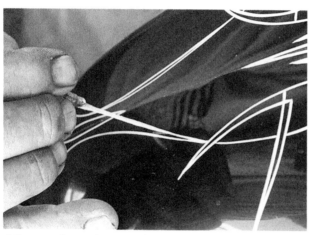

This is where it's critical to make sure your design has a good base and is symmetrical.

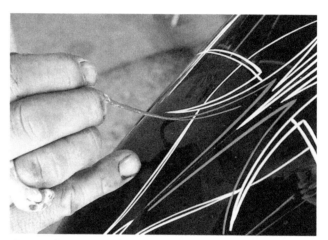

Remember to watch your "guide finger", the first color you laid down, even if after you did the tank you stripped the rest of the white on the bike, this design on the tank will probably still be tacky.

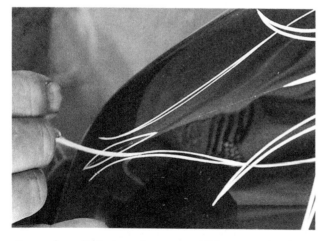

It can be a little busy but, you still have more colors to add so think of how the next color will work with what you are doing now. Think a little ahead.

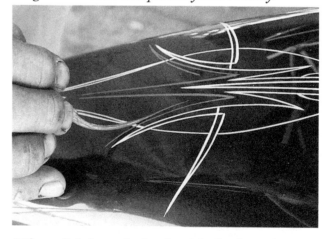

Lift up slightly on the brush while finishing the stroke, this creates the point. All these points should flow together, same style, shape and motion.

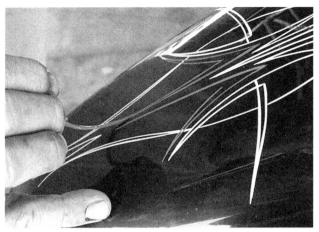

If you are working outside, you will have to thin the paint more often than if you were working inside, especially if it's hot out.

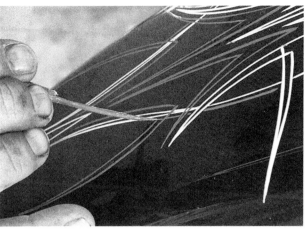

As you are working in the details, make sure you are looking back and forth between the left and right designs to make sure that points, swoops, swirls and lines are even and the same distance apart.

Notice how I use my left hand to support my right hand. You would be surprised at how often this comes into play.

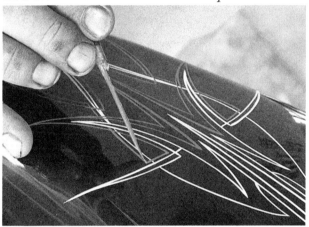

Look at the top of the brush, notice how I have trimmed half of the hair off. This makes the overall length of the hair shorter and better for tight detailed designs.

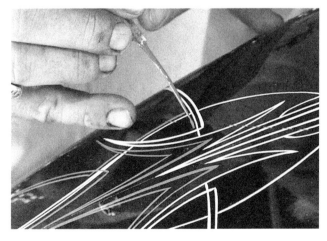

Always think of how you can better your design and only cross the center line when it's necessary or when it's a critical part of the design.

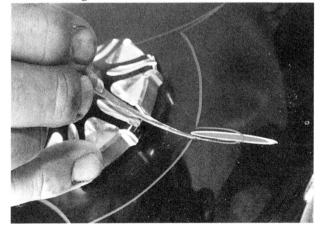

I want to work this design around the gas cap so I can add length to the design. This makes the tank appear longer.

You can't explain this design to a customer. This is why you need to have plenty of books of your work so the customer can see what you are capable of. Maybe even have some different styles that you can do, if they see a style they like and you discuss colors, it's up to you to be creative. Check out the little touches on the turn signals and notice how it mimics the tank design as does the striping on the front fender.

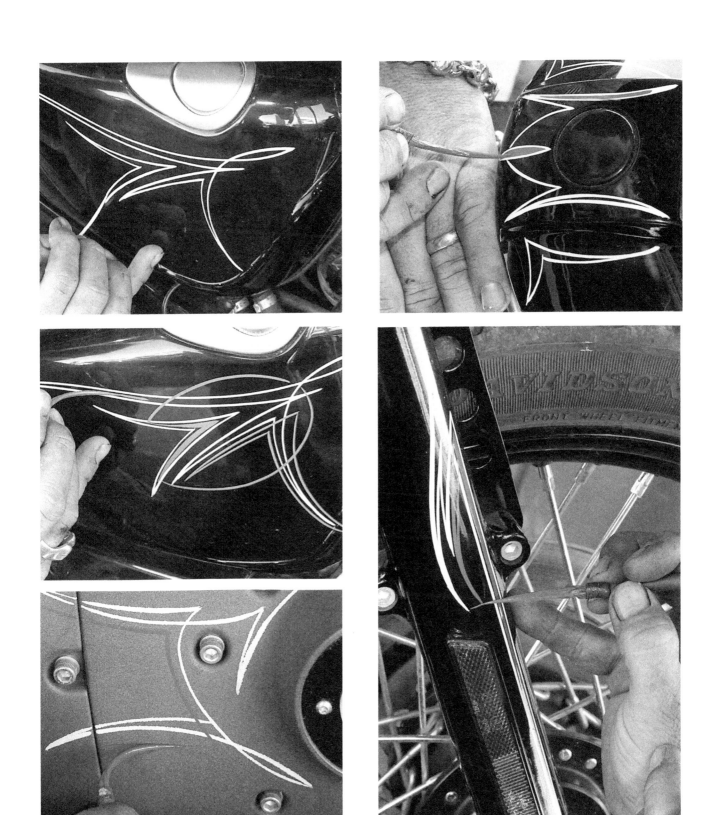

Pinstripes on the oil tank is not out of the ordinary, however, adding touches to the top of the headlight, forks and the primary cover is something that takes "out of the box" thinking. This bike was a little more than what we had discussed, in price, and in the number of designs. I stuck to our original price and did the extra because I wanted to and I thought it was what it needed. This was one of those jobs where the customers appreciate the fact that I gave a little extra.... because I wanted to! Both of the customers in this chapter were great to work with. Occasionally though you get that one customer and you ask yourself if the money is worth it? For me it's not, I'm here to make a living and have fun doing it. Choose wisely.....

Chapter Ten

Mark Brodie

Less Is More

Mark Brodie is one of the lucky ones. A man who found his calling at a young age and never looked back. A man who's just as excited about what he does now, as he was thirty years ago when he was just starting out.

During his thirty year career Mark's been known to paint everything from the hot rods and custom bikes you'd expect, to high-end motorhomes; and his design and paint talents don't stop there. Dale Earnhardt Jr. is a big fan

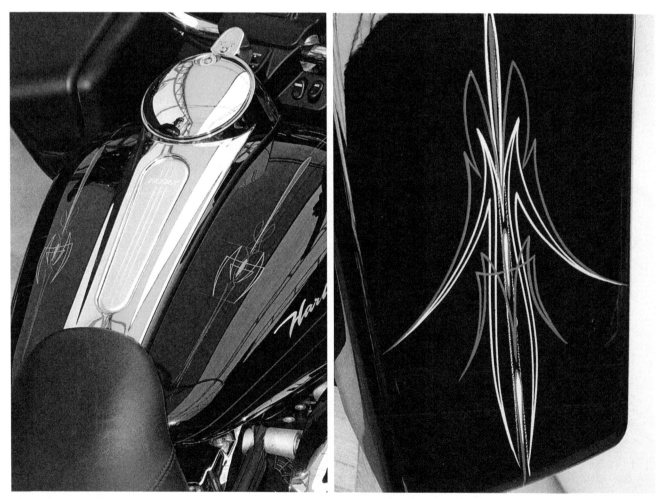

Tank-top art, and a nice set of stripes on a set of bags — both done on a late model Bagger. These are typical of the motorcycle work I've been doing lately.

of Mark Brodie, as was his father. Those are only two of the NASCAR greats who rely on Mark to make their rides stand out from all the rest.

Lest you think everything Mark paints comes with wheels, consider his fine art work, some of the things he paints have heels. His paintings hang in Scottsdale's best galleries, and sell to everyone from home owners to Restaurant owners. There's even a line of Mark Brodie high-heel shoes, the sexiest heels you've ever seen, along with personalized leather vests.

More recently, Mark teamed up with Chester's Harley-Davidson to design a line of Brodie/Chester originals. "We call these Pro Touring bikes," explains Mark. "These are new Harley-Davidsons that you can ride from Phoenix to New York, wash, enter in a bike show, win the show, and then ride home again. Each one is unique, but still very rideable. And we've worked to keep them affordable."

For Mark, what started as an obsession in high school turned into an open-ended career. From canvases that run at two-hundred miles per hour, to those that don't move at all. From cars to clothing, bikes to boutiques, it's been a hell of a ride - and it's not over yet.

Palleting the paint is very important, I'm thinning the paint to a consistency I'm comfortable with. It also depends on the design, thicker is better for small designs while thinner works better for longer lines.

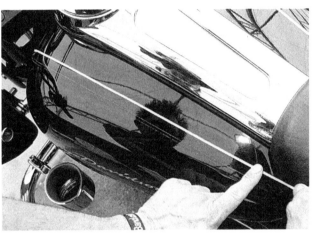

The first thing I do is mark the center of the panel with a piece of 1/8th inch 3M, green masking tape.

Next, I add a set of registration marks, so I can be sure the left and right side designs match each other.

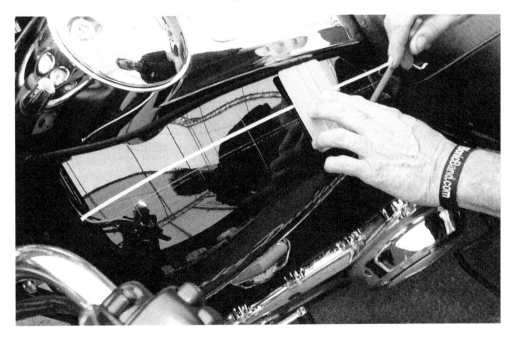

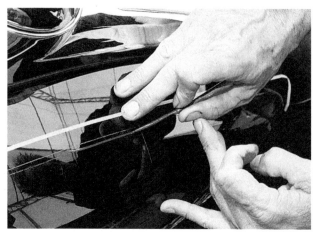

I start the design with a single line…

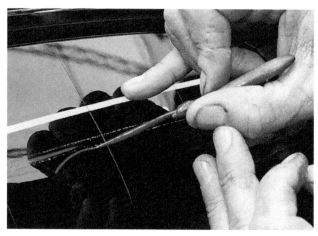

Now I start the lower part of the design with two curves…

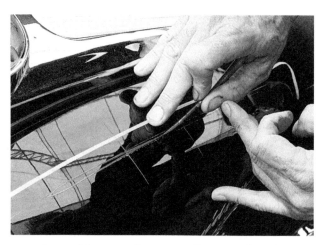

… then add a complimentary line, together they make a long teardrop. I like to use my left hand to steady my brush hand.

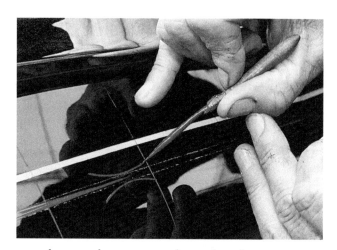

… that together create an hour-glass shape.

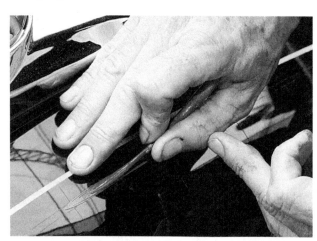

Now I can fill in the teardrop, note how the tape makes a nice guide for my finger. The registration marks help me to be precise in the placement of each part of the design.

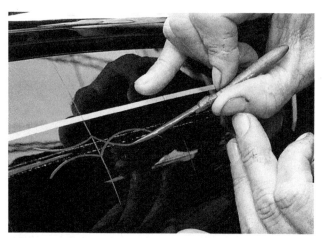

Now I repeat the curves again, but this time they roll the other way.

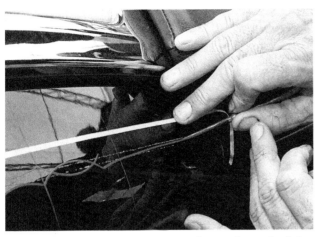

A long spear pulls the design to almost the end of the tank.

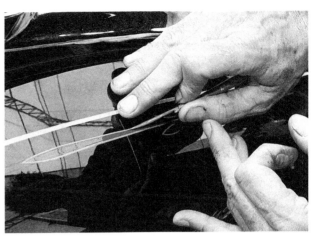

… and also a color the customer wanted.

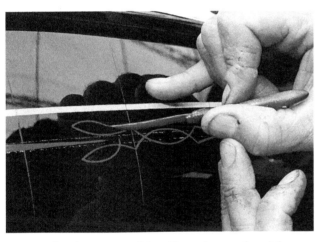

Next I finish up everything I'm going to do with my first color…

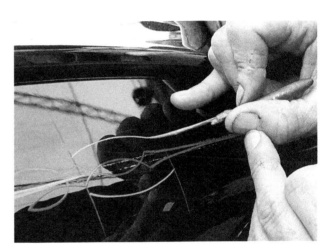

Now I begin adding to the design with my second color.

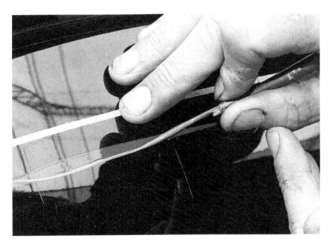

… before adding color number two. The gray is a good choice for this bike…

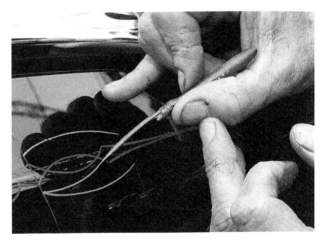

First I go outside…

... then I pull back in...

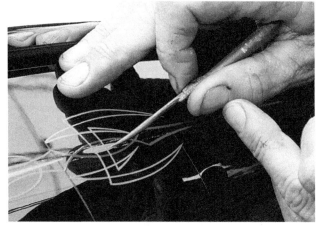

The small teardrop works in harmony with the long red teardrop I placed at the top of the tank.

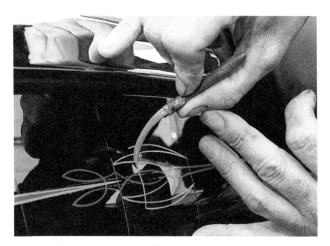

... and across with one horizontal line...

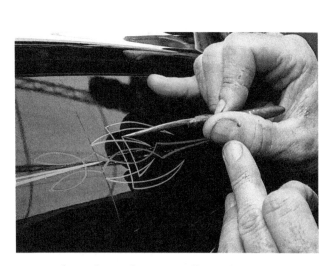

... and another - that tie it all together.

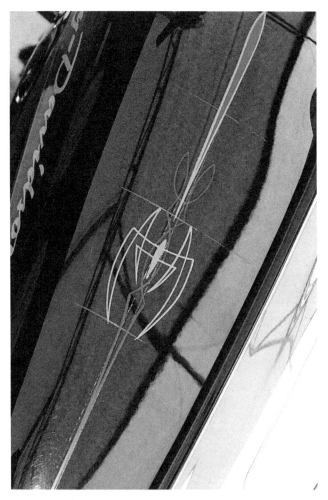

The design is simple and a bit elegant. You don't have to fill up the entire canvas.

Mark Brodie, Q&A

How did you come to be a pinstripe artist?

My Dad owned a car lot, and when I was fourteen years old, he had a pinstripe guy, Able Terrango, some in and do some striping on one of the cars on the lot. I watched him work and I was mesmerized, hooked. I bought a set of brushes the next day.

Dad would bring home a different car home each night, and after dinner I would sneak out to the garage and pinstripe it - and then wipe the stripes off before he saw it. My mom's washer and dryer were good practice canvasses too, metal objects with big flat panels.

By the time I was twenty I was pinstriping for a living, and I'm still at it today.

What do you use for brushes?

I use Mack for intricate design work. The brushes used in the sequences are all Macks, a size 00, trimmed by me. You have to trim the brushes.

That is one of our secrets, you don't use brushes right out of the package. With the Macks, if start with a size 1, you will end up with a 0 or 00.

I like to spin the brush, and take some hairs that stick out from the side. I take a few off the bottom too. When you're done trimming, you should be able to do circles and tight corners without the bristles spraying apart.

How about paint, what are your preferences?

I use One-Shot sometimes. Mostly, though, I use PPG urethane enamel with the hardener. I recommend using the hardener, it's much more durable that way.

Do you clear the pinstripes, do you have any trouble with the clear reacting with the stripes?

I don't deal with it, the clearing. The body shop deals with it. If they are going to clear the stripes though, I make sure I use hardener in the pinstriping paint.

Do you draw out a sketch or design ahead of time?

No, I do not draw any thing out ahead of time. But, I always find the center before I start. Always.

In terms of your designs are there rules you follow, things like the number of times one line can cross another?

There are no rules. It all depends on how you feel. It's about whatever you want at the time, and if the customer gets in the way with what you have planned and wants something else, you tell him, "that won't look good."

Bags of Beauty

Two-Color Pinstripes

The designs seen here are a good example of Mark Brodie putting his money where his mouth is. "The design on these bags just works," explains Mark. "I like fine lines. I tell people, 'You don't have to fill up all the available space. You are just adding color.' The key is to remember: don't overpopulate. Know when to say when. That is vey important."

The stripes are done with one of Mark's favorite brushes, the Mack number 10, trimmed in such a way as to make a good brush even better. Like a lot of pinstripers, Mark often uses both hands, the left becomes a tripod of sorts for the right and helps ensure the lines are clean and straight without even a hint of a wiggle or a ragged edge.

The design itself is pretty simple. A mostly vertical arrangement of lines on a mostly vertical canvas. The bold colors, yellow and red, used on a black bag, ensure that Mark gets the maximum visual impact from a minimal amount of actual paint.

The finished art could easily be placed on a panel that hangs in a gallery, as many of Mark's designs already do. Instead, this intriguing arrangement of yellow and red populate the back panel on two, Harley-Davidson bags. And because the paint is a catalyzed urethane, there's no need to clearcoat the design, the stripes will stand up to all the rain and sun that mother nature can dish out.

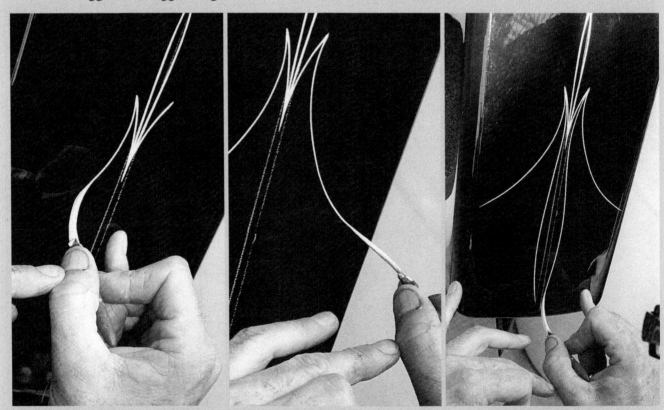

Note the center line...   *...I always do that first...*   *... then I start to layout my design.*

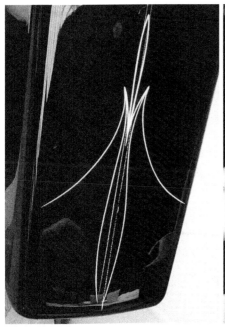

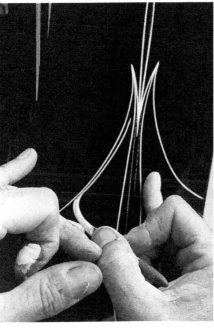

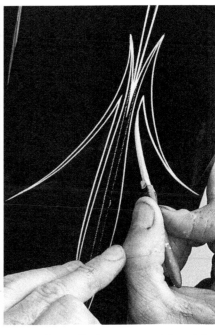

In this case I was looking for colors that really pop...

... the yellow is a good first color. I don't want the design to be completely vertical...

... so I've pulled it out to either side, before...

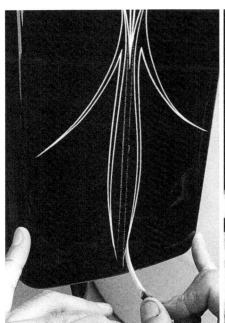

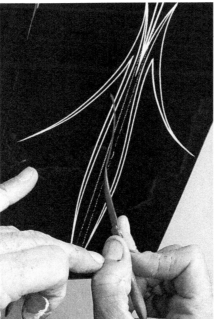

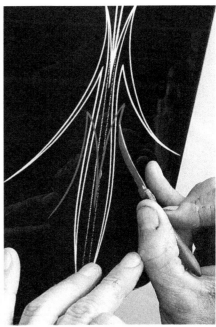

... pulling the lines down to tie in with what I've already done.

A second color, bright red in this case...

... gives the design a lot more visual impact.

141

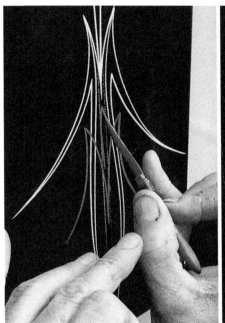

In situations like this…

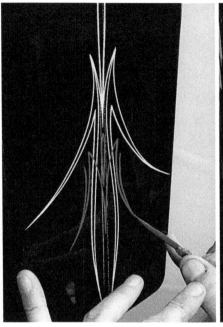

… I'm careful to keep my supporting fingers out of the wet paint.

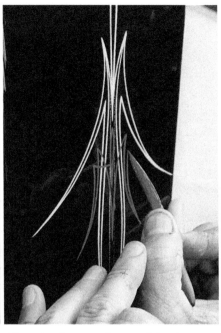

You also have to be careful when crossing one line with another…

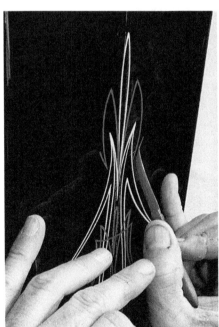

That you don't smear the paint as you pull a wet brush across the still-wet lines you just put down.

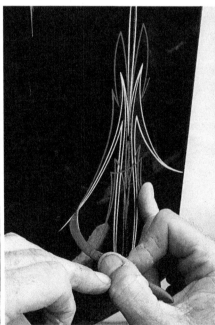

Part of the trick is to make sure the paint is the right viscosity…

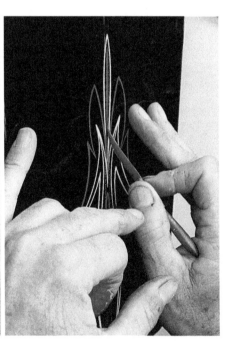

… if the paint on the brush is too wet and runny it will smear the lines.

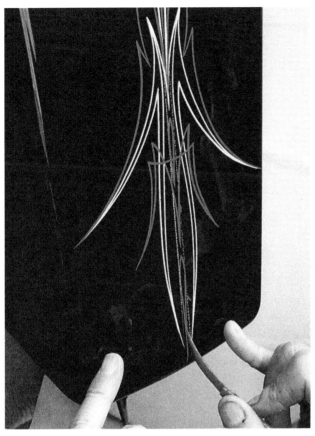

The design done in red really mimicks what I did in yellow. I like lines that are thin and consistent.

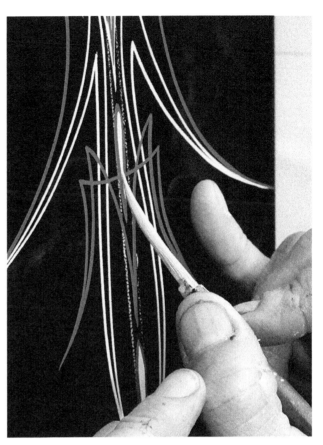

Teardrops done in one color and outlined with another pop like neon lights.

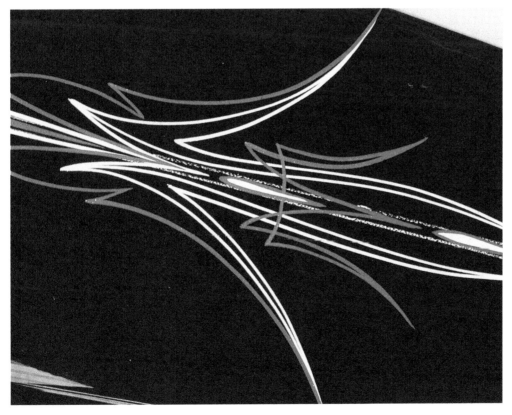

Like I said, you don't have to fill the entire canvas. Open space surrounding the pinstripes makes it easier to see and fully appreciate the design. It's important to know when to say when.

Sources

Andy Anderson
Anderson Studio Inc
2609 Grissom Dr.
Nashville, TN 37204
615-255-4807
www.andersonstudioinc.com

Mark Brodie
Mark Brodie Motorsports Inc.
Phoenix, AZ
480-634-5939
www.markbrodieinc.com
mark@markbrodieinc.com

Kelley St. Croix-Bush
Wizard Custom Studios and St.
Croix Airbrushing
230 2nd Ave W.
Milltown, WI 54858
763-238-2400

Leah and Brian Gall
Finishline Custom Paint
& Design Inc.
21725 Co. Rd. 10
Corcoran, MN 55374
763-416-4371
getgraphx@aol.com
www.finishlinecustompaint.com
facebook.com/finishlinecustom-
paint

Nub Graphix
www.nubgrafix.com/
info@nubgraphics.com

Mickey Harris
P.O. Box 384
Cosby, TN 37722
mickey @ mickeyharrisart.com
mickeyharrisart.com
Tracy Hilgers,
TJ Design
20751 Helena Blvd
Jordan, MN 55352
952-492-5097
www.custombikepaint.com
tj@custombikepaint.com

House of Kolor
800-845-2500
www.houseofkolor.com
houseofkolor@valspar.com

Dave Letterfly
www.letterfly.com
artists@letterfly.com
813-752-8063

One-Shot
1701 East 122nd St.
Chicago, IL 60633
773-646-2778
www.1shot.com

PPG
www.ppgrefinish.com

Tex McDorman
Tex Efx
6200 Crow Wright Rd.
Sanger, Texas 76266
940-482-9969
tex@texefx.com
www.Texefx.com
Saral Paper Company
400 East 55th Street, Suite 18B
New York, NY 10022
Phone: 212-223-3322
lambaster@aol.com
www.saralpaper.com/products.html

SATA
Dan-Am Company
Exclusive independent distributor
of SATA in the USA &
Puerto Rico.
www.satausa.com
One SATA Dr.
POB 46
Spring Valley, MN 55975

Lenni Schwartz
Krazy Kolors
5413 Helena Rd N.
Oakdale MN 55128
651-773-9015
krazykolors@msn.com

CPSIA information can be obtained
at www.ICGtesting.com
Printed in the USA
BVOW07s1040190516
448744BV00018B/34/P